# Priests Today

# Priests
# Today
## Reflections on
## Identity, Life,
## and Ministry

edited by
**Brendan Leahy & Michael Mulvey**

NEW CITY PRESS
Hyde Park, NY

Published in the United States by New City Press
202 Comforter Blvd., Hyde Park, NY 12538
www.newcitypress.com
©2010 New City Press

Cover design by Leandro de Leon

Library of Congress Cataloging-in-Publication Data:

Priests today : reflections on identity, life, and ministry / Brendan Leahy
and Michael Mulvey (eds.).
    p. cm.
  Includes bibliographical references.
  ISBN 978-1-56548-346-0 (pbk. : alk. paper)  1.  Priesthood—Catholic
Church—Meditations. 2.  Catholic Church—Clergy—Religious life—
Meditations.  I. Leahy, Breandan, 1960- II. Mulvey, Michael, Rev.
  BX1912.5.P75 2010
  242'.802—dc22                                              2009048900

Printed in the United States of America

# Contents

# Preface

When the late Cardinal van Thuan was imprisoned in solitary confinement in Vietnam for 14 years, it seemed all possibilities of a fruitful priestly ministry had vanished. Yet later, in recalling how he managed to open up a dialogue with his prison guards and fellow prisoners, many of them Buddhist, and how every day, with three drops of wine and a drop of water in the palm of his hand, he would celebrate Mass, he spoke enthusiastically of those challenging years as very special years of priesthood.

For many priests today, the sense of challenge is great. Some feel caught between an old order of pre-Vatican II times and an attempted new post-conciliar order. The storm of scandals relating to clerical abuse has clearly taken its toll on priests too. On top of this, it seems they have an increasingly endless round of groups to meet, committees to sit on and projects often not of their devising to accompany. And all this with fewer colleagues! They would not be human if at times they didn't experience moments of discouragement.

That is why, perhaps as never before, priests, "ministers of the sacred," and indeed all members of the Church, need from time to time to help one another rediscover the spark of inspiration and enthusiasm that lies at the heart of priestly ministry and life. In this book of reflections, we have chosen texts that we believe open windows onto aspects of spirituality and pastoral ministry that encourage and prompt renewal.

What lies behind our selection is the conviction that it is above all in a life of communion with others, understood and lived out in a robust spirituality of communion, that priests can find new hope and strength as they interrelate with their parishioners, with their brother priests, with their bishops and with all who pass them by, moment by moment, in ministry and life.

*Brendan Leahy and Michael Mulvey*

# 1

# Believing in God Who Is Love

........................

1  *A New Horizon*

........................

"God is love, and he who abides in love abides in God, and God abides in him" (1 Jn 4:16). These words from the First Letter of John express with remarkable clarity the heart of the Christian faith: the Christian image of God and the resulting image of humankind and its destiny. In the same verse, Saint John also offers a kind of summary of the Christian life: "We have come to know and to believe in the love God has for us."

*We have come to believe in God's love*: in these words the Christian can express the fundamental decision of his life. Being Christian is not the result of an ethical choice or a lofty idea, but the encounter with an event, a person, which gives life a new horizon and a decisive direction....

Since God has first loved us (cf. 1 Jn 4:10), love is now no longer a mere "command"; it is the response to the gift of love with which God draws near to us.

*Pope Benedict XVI*

............................

2   *Wondrous Exchange*

............................

The priestly vocation is a mystery. *It is the mystery of a "wondrous exchange" — admirabile commercium —* between God and man. A man offers his humanity to Christ, so that Christ may use him as an instrument of salvation, making him as it were into another Christ. Unless we grasp the mystery of this "exchange," we will not understand how it can be that a young man, hearing the words "Follow me!," can give up everything for Christ, in the certainty that if he follows this path he will find complete personal fulfillment.

*Pope John Paul II*

...................................

3   *A Continual "Yes" to God*

...................................

The call of God is one of the most beautiful things on this earth. Think of the interweaving of divine and human love involved in a vocation. When God calls us to a particular way of life, he looks on us with his love: the moment we become aware of it a new life begins for us. Even before we were born, God was looking at us and loving us in the setting he had always planned for us. In fact, he brought us into being to put his plan for us into operation....

Anyone who hears his call often feels fear, and even doubts or terror, but when he discovers its implications, he also feels joy. So the most beautiful moment is not when a person hears the call, but when he says "yes" making God's call real, his will clinging to God's. It is an allegiance for life, a continual "yes" to God who repeats the invitation for ever.

*Pasquale Foresi*

## 4   *God before Everything and Everyone*

Apart from the good God ... nothing is stable, nothing, nothing! If it is life, it passes; if it is fortune, it crumbles; if it is health, it is destroyed; if it is reputation, it is severely tarnished. We pass like the wind.... Everything goes quickly, everything is blown away.

Oh, my God, my God! How much are to be pitied those who place their affection in all kinds of things!... They place it there because they love themselves too much; but they do not love with a rational love; they love with love for themselves and for the world, seeking themselves, seeking creatures more than God. They are never satisfied therefore, they are never peaceful; they are always worried, always tormented, always overwhelmed.

*Saint John Mary Vianney*

## 5 The "Emptiness Filled"

Dear co-workers of Christ, you have said "Yes" to Jesus and he has taken you at your word. The Word of God became Jesus, the poor one. Your celibacy is the terrible emptiness you experience. God cannot fill what is full; he can fill only emptiness … It is not how much we really "have" to give, but how empty we are — so that we can receive fully in our life and let him live his life in us.

In you, today, he wants to relive his complete submission to his Father. Allow him to do so. It does not matter what you feel, but what he feels in you….

Take away your eyes from yourself and rejoice that you have nothing, that you are nothing, that you can do nothing. Give Jesus a big smile, each time your nothingness frightens you.… You and I must let him live in us and through us in the world. Cling to Our Lady, for she too, before she could become full of grace, full of Jesus, had to go through that darkness. How could this be done? She asked. But the moment she said "yes" she had need to go in haste to give Jesus to John and his family.

*Mother Teresa*

## 6   *It Is the "How" that Counts*

$S$ome days things seem to go well, humanly speaking, and there are those days when things go less well. And then you happily repeat the experience in this present life that what counts is not whether the day goes better or worse, but *how* you live this life, because in the *how* is charity, which alone gives value to all things. The one who loves God is the one who keeps his word (see Jn 14:23).

Each day we should recall that in paradise we will bring with us neither our joys nor our sorrows. Even if we hand over our bodies to be burned, without charity it amounts to nothing (see 1 Cor 13:3). Neither do apostolic works have value. Not even the ability to speak in angelic tongues, without charity, counts for anything (see 1 Cor 13:1).

Nor do the works of mercy. Even giving away all we have to the poor, without charity, counts for nothing (see 1 Cor 13:3).

We will carry to paradise how we have lived all this: whether we have lived in accord with the word of God, which gives us the means to express our charity.

So, let us get up cheerfully each day be it stormy or sunny, and let us remember that our day will be worthwhile to the extent that during it we have "assimilated" the word of God. Living like this during the day, Christ will have been living in us and he will have given value to everything we have done by our direct action or by our contribution of prayer and suffering. And these, in the end, will follow us (see Rev 14:13).

*Chiara Lubich*

.........................

## 7   *A Decision for Life*

.........................

Just think: You took on the priesthood as a final decision for life. You can no longer go back on this decision; you must sustain it through all the periods of life that you do not and cannot yet know.… Here we should and must have the courage to live another life, the life of inner continuity, of "growth," of the inner relatedness of the different phases and periods of life to one another and also to the unity of life: with its "yes," with its decision and with what comes later, although we do not yet know it. Experience of the apostolate at thirty is something quite different from the experience at sixty.… Can we nevertheless say "yes"? We can. Why? Because God has guaranteed through his Spirit in the church to sustain us with his grace, if only we do our part, if we manage to imitate and realize afresh the one, continuous growth of Christ, simply as man, unfolding it in the unity of one life.

*Karl Rahner*

........................................

## 8   *God and not God's Works*

........................................

During my long nine-year ordeal of solitary confinement, I was in a cell without windows. For days at a time the electric lights were left on day and night; and then for days at a time there was complete darkness. I felt as though I were suffocating from the heat and humidity to the point of insanity.… I could not sleep because I was so tormented by the thought of being forced to abandon my diocese, and of the many works that I had begun for God now going to ruin.… One night, from the depths of my heart, a voice said to me, "Why do you torment yourself like this? You must distinguish between God and the works of God. Everything you have done and desire to continue doing — pastoral visits, formation of seminarians, of men and women religious, of the youth, construction of schools, *foyers* for students, missions for the evangelization of non-Christians — all of these are excellent works, but they are works of God, *they* are not God! God … will entrust his works to others that are much more capable. You have chosen God alone, not his works!"

This light gave me a new peace.…

*Cardinal Francis Xavier Van Thuan*

..................................

9  *Prayer of Abandonment*

..................................

Father,
I abandon myself into your hands; do with me
  what you will.
Whatever you may do, I thank you:
I am ready for all, I accept all.
Let only your will be done in me, and in all your
  creatures.
I wish no more than this, O Lord.
Into your hands I commend my soul;
I offer it to you
with all the love of my heart,
for I love you, Lord,
and so need to give myself,
to surrender myself into your hands,
without reserve,
and with boundless confidence,
for you are my Father.

*Charles de Foucauld*

# 2
# Following Jesus

10 *Professionals of the Sacred?*

No one is closer to his master than the servant who has access to the most private dimensions of his life. In this sense "to serve" means closeness, it requires familiarity. This familiarity also bears a danger: when we continually encounter the sacred it risks becoming habitual for us. In this way, reverential fear is extinguished. Conditioned by all our habits we no longer perceive the great, new and surprising fact that he himself is present, speaks to us, gives himself to us. We must ceaselessly struggle against this becoming accustomed to the extraordinary reality, against the indifference of the heart, always recognizing our insufficiency anew and the grace that there is in the fact that he consigned himself into our hands.

*Pope Benedict XVI*

........................................

## 11 *Just as the Father Sent Me ...*

........................................

Among the divine words Jesus uttered, there is one that makes us dizzy when we think it was pronounced by God, and helps us to understand the privilege of election. It is a paradoxical comparison, while at the same time true and deeply mysterious. Christ directs these words to those who over the centuries were to be his priests: "Just as the Father sent me, I send you." Who then, is a priest? A person chosen by Christ to continue his presence in time.

Unfortunately priests are often not like this. But if on the other hand, they are not Christ, they are very little indeed. Their sermons are empty words and their churches are deserted. For the word that Christ gave was He himself.

If the priest first of all lives what he preaches and then speaks, his word will be Christ and he too will be another Christ. His talks will attract the crowds and the churches will be full to the brim. What makes a priest is not knowledge, but the charism brought to life with love.

*Chiara Lubich*

## 12 *The Evangelical Counsels*

It is a fact that for too long, Christians have considered the evangelical counsels to be the private prerogative of consecrated religious life. We used to say, "They are great, the evangelical counsels, but just for religious life; Christians — or diocesan priests — who live in the world, need another style, another spirituality." But the evangelical counsels are not at all a devotional practice or an ascetic invention reserved to a few; they are obligatory and vital methods for accepting with our lives the invitation to be, as Christians, followers of Jesus.

This was never a theoretical question for Jesus. He said, "Whoever wants to be a follower of mine, and does not leave father, mother, brothers, sisters, wives, children, fields … ; who does not deny himself, his own life, cannot be my disciple." He spoke in this way to those who wanted to follow him; he spoke in this way to those who wanted to be Christians. It is the basic condition for beginning the adventure of following him. If we want to be true disciples of Christ, we cannot proceed simply ignoring the evangelical counsels.

*Silvano Cola*

## 13 *Trial of Love*

Following the example of Jesus, *the priest*, "administrator of the mysteries of God," is himself, *when he is "for others."* Prayer gives him a particular sensitivity to these others, making him attentive to their needs, to their life and their destiny. Prayer permits a priest to recognize those that "the Father has given him."

They are those, principally, who the Good Shepherd has placed along the way of his priestly service, *of his pastoral care....* They are those who are spiritually close, disposed to collaborate in the apostolic work, but they are also those who are far away, the absent, the indifferent, those who are pondering or who are looking for something.

How can he be "for" all of these, and "for" each of them, according to Christ's model? How can he be "for" those that *"the Father gives to us,"* entrusting them to us as a commitment? Ours will always be a *test of love* — a test that we have to accept, first of all, in the aspect of prayer....

And when it seems that the test is more than we can bear, let us remember what the Evangelist says about Jesus in Gethsemane, *"in his anguish he prayed even more earnestly"* (Lk 22:44).

*Pope John Paul II*

## 14 *Your Own Home Everywhere*

Whoever follows Jesus, does not do so in order to live in a particular place (a presbytery for example).... Whoever follows Jesus follows God, and therefore has no place except in God himself.

If, on the one hand, this might seem negative, a renunciation of everything, on the other hand it can also be viewed in a positive sense. Every place in the world, all the houses in the world, become ours, because the Son of Man is master of the universe and his home cannot just be a little house in a little town.

Whoever follows Jesus finds his home everywhere, finds his town everywhere, and similarly finds his family and his homeland everywhere.

This is an overwhelming aspect of a vocation: we do not follow Jesus in a particular place, in a particular house; we follow Jesus in order to be his children and his brothers throughout the whole universe.

*Pasquale Foresi*

.........................

15 *Problems Simplified*

.........................

$M$y soul is gravely ill. Yesterday, when just back from Rome, all I heard about was difficulties: the problem of the seminary, the problem of the Congregation for the Cause of Saints, etc., and I got a headache. What came to mind, however, was that I am not the real bishop of this diocese, the real bishop is Jesus. He gave me the problems, so he will also give me the solutions.

I surely have to do all my part too. I must be an instrument of his truth, his goodness and his love. In the evening I renewed my decision to tend towards sanctity. I must not slacken my prayer life the way I do. I must die each day. I must die each day with Christ.

If I make this resolution and act on it, my problems will be simplified. Let us tend towards holiness. The Pope urged us bishops to do this last May.

*Cardinal Stefano Kim*

............................

## 16 *My Vocation Is Love*

............................

"I feel in me the vocation of the Priest. With what love, O Jesus, I would carry You in my hands when, at my voice, You would come down from heaven. And with what love I would give you to souls....

I understood that Love comprised all vocations, that love was everything, that it embraced all times and places ... in a word that it was eternal! Then in the excess of my delirious joy, I cried out: O Jesus, my Love ... my vocation, at last I have found it.... My vocation is love! Yes, I have found my place in the Church and it is You, O my God, who has given me this place; in the heart of the Church, my Mother, I shall be Love. Thus I shall be everything, and thus my dream will be realized.

*Thérèse of Lisieux*

............................

## 17 *Fulfilled in Our "Yes"*

............................

Being united to Christ calls for renunciation. It means not wanting to impose our own way and our own will, not desiring to become someone else, but abandoning ourselves to him, however and wherever he wants to use us.... In the words "I do," spoken at our priestly ordination, we made this fundamental renunciation of our desire to be independent, "self-made." But day by day this great "yes" has to be lived out in the many little "yes-es" and small sacrifices. This "yes" made up of tiny steps which together make up the great "yes," can be lived out without bitterness and self-pity only if Christ is truly the center of our lives. If we enter into true closeness to him. Then indeed we experience, amid sacrifices which can at first be painful, the growing joy of friendship with him, and all the small and sometimes great signs of his love, which he is constantly showing us. "The one who loses himself, finds himself." When we dare to lose ourselves for the Lord, we come to experience the truth of these words.

*Pope Benedict XVI*

..................

18  *"Show" Jesus*

..................

"We wish to see Jesus" (Jn 12:21). This request, addressed to the Apostle Philip by some Greeks who had made a pilgrimage to Jerusalem for the Passover, echoes spiritually in our ears too during this Jubilee Year. Like those pilgrims of two thousand years ago, the men and women of our own day — often perhaps unconsciously — ask believers not only to "speak" of Christ, but in a certain sense to "show" him to them. And is it not the Church's task to reflect the light of Christ in every historical period, to make his face shine also before the generations of the new millennium?

*Pope John Paul II*

. . . . . . . . . . . . . . . . . . . . . . . . . . . . . . . . . . . . . . .

## 19 *Christ in Me Loves Christ in You*

. . . . . . . . . . . . . . . . . . . . . . . . . . . . . . . . . . . . . . .

"In the history of Christian spirituality it was said: 'Christ is in me, he lives in me,' and that is the perspective of individual spirituality, life in Christ. When it also was said: 'Christ is present in my brothers,' this develops the perspective of works of charity, but it falls short of saying that if Christ is in me and Christ is in you, then Christ in me loves Christ in you and vice versa … which would involve a mutual giving and receiving." In a spirituality of communion, one goes towards heaven not only with others but also through and in others. If God comes down to earth through his Son made flesh, then we ascend towards heaven through Jesus present in each sister and brother for whom he died.

*Thomas J. Norris*
*(quoting Jesús Castellano Cervera)*

# 3

# Making the Church the Home and School of Communion

To make the Church the *home and the school of communion*: that is the great challenge facing us in the millennium which is now beginning, if we wish to be faithful to God's plan and respond to the world's deepest yearnings.

But what does this mean in practice? Here too, our thoughts could run immediately to the action to be undertaken, but that would not be the right impulse to follow. Before making practical plans, we need to *promote a spirituality of communion*, making it the guiding principle of education wherever individuals and Christians are formed, wherever ministers of the altar, consecrated persons, and pastoral workers are trained, wherever families and communities are being built up....

Let us have no illusions: unless we follow this spiritual path, external structures of communion will serve very little purpose. They would become mechanisms without a soul, "masks" of communion rather than its means of expression and growth.

*Pope John Paul II*

........................................................

21 *Royal Priesthood, Ministerial Priesthood*

........................................................

Therefore all the disciples of Christ, persevering in prayer and praising God (cf. Acts 2:42–47) should present themselves as a living sacrifice, holy and pleasing to God (cf. Rm 12:1). Everywhere on earth they must bear witness to Christ and give an answer to those who seek an account of that hope of eternal life which is in them (cf. 1Pt 3:15).

Though they differ from one another in essence and not only in degree, the common priesthood of the faithful and the ministerial or hierarchical priest-hood are nonetheless interrelated: each of them in its own special way is a participation in the one priest-hood of Christ.

The ministerial priest, by the sacred power he enjoys, teaches and rules the priestly people; acting in the person of Christ, he makes present the Eu-charistic sacrifice, and offers it to God in the name of all the people. But the faithful, in virtue of their royal priesthood, join in the offering of the Eucharist. They likewise exercise that priesthood in receiving the sacraments, in prayer and thanksgiving, in the witness of a holy life, and by self-denial and active charity.

*Second Vatican Council*

....................................

## 22 *Two Kinds of Priesthood*

....................................

Some commentators have had difficulty about the statement of LG 10 that the two kinds of priesthood in the church differ not only in degree but in essence, but the statement is clear and helpful so far as it goes. It obviously does not mean that the ordained priest undergoes an essential change, thereby ceasing to be a partaker in our common humanity. The distinction is not between two kinds of persons but two kinds of priesthood. The council refuses to attribute a higher grade or degree to the ministerial, as though the common priesthood ranked lower than it on the same scale. Instead, it situates the two kinds of priesthood in different categories, like oranges and apples. The ministerial priesthood involves a public representational function rather than a personal giftedness. It anything, the common priesthood is more exalted, for the ministers are ordained for the sake of service toward the whole people of God.

*Avery Dulles*

## 23 *States of Life in Relation with One Another*

Each (way of living the universal vocation to sanctity) has a basic and unmistakable character which sets each apart, while at the same time each of them is seen in relation to the other and placed at each other's service.

Thus the *lay* state of life has its distinctive feature in its secular character. It fulfills an ecclesial service in bearing witness and, in its own way recalling for priests, women and men religious, the significance of the earthly and temporal realities in the salvific plan of God. In turn, the *ministerial* priesthood represents in different times and places, the permanent guarantee of the sacramental presence of Christ, the Redeemer. The *religious* state bears witness to the eschatological character of the Church, that is, the straining towards the Kingdom of God that is prefigured and in some way anticipated and experienced even now through the vows of chastity, poverty and obedience.

All the states of life, whether taken collectively or individually in relation to the others, are at the service of the Church's growth. While different in expression they are deeply united in the Church's "mystery of communion" and are dynamically coordinated in its unique mission.

*Pope John Paul II*

## 24 *"For You, with You"*

$O$rdination brings the one being ordained into a fundamentally new ecclesial relationship, beyond that established by Christian initiation. Moreover, this new ecclesial relationship, established through sacramental ordination, cannot imply the renunciation of the relation established in Christian initiation. The demands of baptism continue for the ordained. What results from sacramental ordination is a twofold relation. St. Augustine articulated this quite well in one of his sermons: "What I should be for you fills me with anguish; what I can be with you is my consolation; because for you I am a bishop, but with you a Christian. The first points to my duty, the second to grace. The first shows the danger, the other salvation." Note that the prepositions "for" and "with" signify the dual relations established by ordination and baptism. Both Christian initiation and ordination can be considered adequately only from within this relational ecclesiology of communion.

*Richard R. Gaillardetz*

## 25 *A Rich Network of Relationships*

The identity of each Christian, and hence the specific identity of the priest and his ministry, is revealed within the mystery of the Church, a mystery of Trinitarian communion in a missionary tension....

This is how we can understand the essentially "relational" meaning of the priestly identity. Through the priesthood, which springs forth from the depths of the ineffable mystery of God, ... the priest is placed in a sacramental way in communion with the bishop and the other priests in order to serve the People of God and the Church and to draw everyone to Christ, according to the Lord's prayer: "... may they all be one, as we are one...."

It is impossible, therefore, to define the nature and mission of the priestly mission, except in the context of this rich network of relationships, which spring forth from the Most Holy Trinity and are continued in the communion of the Church, as a sign and instrument in Christ of union with God and of the unity of the whole human race.

*Pope John Paul II*

A spirituality of communion also means an ability to think of our brothers and sisters in faith within the profound unity of the Mystical Body, and therefore as "those who are a part of me." This makes us able to share their joys and sufferings, to sense their desires and attend to their needs, to offer them deep and genuine friendship. A spirituality of communion implies also the ability to see what is positive in others, to welcome it and prize it as a gift from God: not only as a gift for the brother or sister who has received it directly, but also as a "gift for me." A spirituality of communion means, finally, to know how to "make room" for our brothers and sisters, bearing "each other's burdens" (Gal 6:2) and resisting the selfish temptations which constantly beset us and provoke competition, careerism, distrust and jealousy.

*Pope John Paul II*

## 27 Co-Responsible Lay People

It is necessary to improve pastoral structures in such a way that the co-responsibility of all the members of the People of God in their entirety is gradually promoted, with respect for vocations and for the respective roles of the consecrated and of lay people.

This demands a change in mindset, particularly concerning lay people. They must no longer be viewed as "collaborators" of the clergy but truly recognized as "co-responsible," for the Church's being and action, thereby fostering the consolidation of a mature and committed laity. This common awareness of being Church of all the baptized in no way diminishes the responsibility of parish priests. It is precisely your task, dear parish priests, to nurture the spiritual and apostolic growth of those who are already committed to working hard in the parishes. They form the core of the community that will act as a leaven for the others.

*Pope Benedict XVI*

## 28  *Disciples and Brothers*

Though priests of the New Testament, in virtue of the sacrament of Orders, exercise the most outstanding and necessary office of father and teacher among and for the People of God, they are nevertheless, together with all Christ's faithful, disciples of the Lord, made sharers in his Kingdom by the grace of God's call. For priests are brothers among brothers and sisters with all those who have been reborn at the baptismal font. They are all members of one and the same Body of Christ, the building up of which is required of everyone.

Priests, therefore, must take the lead in seeking the things of Jesus Christ, not the things that are their own. They must work together with the lay faithful, and conduct themselves in their midst after the example of their Master, who among us "came not to be ministered unto, but to minister, and to give his life as redemption for many" (Mt 20:28).

*Second Vatican Council*

## 29 *Group or "Community"?*

$W$hen community life in the seminary is considered only a means in order to reach a goal, there's a strong risk that seminarians remain a "group," simply come together "for" something. Interpersonal communion is not made a priority and so the classmate remains a classmate, the formator remains a formator and not the "neighbor" with whom one has, above all, to establish a real reciprocity of love ("Above all else ... have mutual love among you" [1 Pet 4:8]).

The result is that Christian community is not created, there's no experience of that "civilization" of heaven which is Trinitarian communion.

If Jesus asks above all for mutual love it is because it is the first and fundamental value also for human co-existence which cannot but be a reflection of the life of the Trinity, its ultimate model.

Without ... mutual love sooner or later an existential emptiness sets in and everything loses value. Even the vocation itself weakens and co-existence becomes a penance while studies, lacking the light of Wisdom, become sterile professionalism.

*Silvano Cola*

The church is not an administration like any other administration, even though it must have its structures and instruments of dialogue and policy making. An administration is always the construct of its managers. The Church is the place where we encounter God's action.... Renewal in the Church is never something external or superficial. It is never just a process about committees and working groups. It is rather a process of renewed understanding and of meaning. It involves a community day by day — in the changed and challenging situation of the world in which we live — entering into the mystery of the Word made flesh in order to see how we can sanctify the world around us, in all its corporeity, its bodiliness, in its concrete expressions.... The parish must appear to outsiders as a place where people gather together not just to carry out ritual and return back to their individual concerns. Parish must be a place where people encounter a different relationship between people.... Enhancing the place of the laity, women and men, in the Church will also enhance the specific vocation and service of the priest, who is chosen to ensure that the Church can celebrate "in memory of me" and in "the person of Christ" the saving actions of Jesus Christ.

*Archbishop Diarmuid Martin*

If you are in class, recognize one another; if you are in the store, recognize one another; if you are in the housing estate, recognize one another; if you are in the parish, recognize one another: you are members of one another if you are members of Christ. This is the most revolutionary sentence that can be expressed: "you are members of one another."

That's how Mother Teresa of Calcutta sees the man out in the open, in the sewer, who is dirty and indeed "debris," and welcomes him as a member of Christ, that is, hers. And this recognizing one another must be seen. If it is not seen by others then it doesn't exist, it is not true. It must be seen because this is witness to Christ. This is the first expression of our yearning for Christ.

*Luigi Giussani*

The shepherds are not separated from the flock, they form part of it, subject like the rest to all the exigencies of the Christian vocation....

As to the common priesthood, to reduce it to the practice of individual worship would be to distort it … since Christian worship consists in transforming the world by means of divine love, its principal task is to establish and promote communion. When the priestly people unites itself through a life of love with the action of Christ's offering, it releases a dynamic of love which spreads throughout the world and progressively transforms it.

It is clear that this task has more connection with mediation than with ritual offerings in the manner of the Old Testament worship. However, it can only be accomplished through the priestly mediation of Christ, and this can only be accepted when it is made visible. This is the reason for a ministry in which this mediation is rendered visible and efficacious.

*Albert Vanhoye*

# 4
# Reaching Out to Everyone

......................

## 33  *Unity with All*

......................

1.  It is necessary with God's help to live in the
    service of unity, to be in love with this, to be
    servants of unity, its apostles, prophets and
    martyrs. And so in those places where we live
    and work, where God places us:
    a.  The need to say or do nothing that would
        be a cause of disunity or would promote
        intrigues, mistrust or coldness.
    b.  Attentiveness to not letting yourself be
        drawn along by the father of evil and his
        messengers that sometimes can be good
        and virtuous people used by the Evil
        One.
    c.  The joy of resolving arguments, promot-
        ing union, helping people see the good
        side of others, serving dialogue.
2.  To be complete, the thirst for unity must include all
    people of all times, places, races, parties and creeds.

*Dom Helder Camara*

## 34 As Yourself

Every Word of God contains both the minimum and the maximum that he can ask of you, so when you read, "Love your neighbor as yourself" (Mt 19:19), you have the law of fraternal love at its highest degree.

Your neighbor is another you, and you must love him or her bearing that in mind.

When neighbors cry, you must cry with them, and when they laugh, laugh with them. If they lack knowledge, be ignorant with them. If they have lost a parent, make their suffering your own.

You and they are members of Christ and if one or the other is suffering, it is the same for you.

What has value for you is *God* who is both their Father and yours.

Do not seek to be excused from loving. Your neighbors are those who pass next to you, be they rich or poor, beautiful or not, brilliant or not, holy or sinful, a fellow citizen or a foreigner, a priest or layperson, whoever.

Try to love whoever appears to you in the present moment of your life. You will discover within yourself an energy and strength you did not know you had. It will add flavor to your life, and you will find answers to your thousand questions why.

*Chiara Lubich*

## 35 *In the "Total" Family*

The man who is ordained priest ... leaves his home and the world becomes his home. His father, mother, and brothers are no longer only, and not chiefly, those people whose blood he shares, but are those whose condition he shares: the least ... the disinherited, the unknown, the poor that no one sees. He leaves his particular family to become a minister of the total family.

*Igino Giordani*


## 36 *The Poor as Companions*

The Church is called to be "advocate of justice and of the poor" before the "intolerable social and economic inequalities" that "cry to heaven...." [The preferential option for the poor] means it must pervade all our pastoral structures and priorities. The Church is called to be the sacrament of love, solidarity and justice....

This permanent outlook is needed, one that is made manifest in concrete choices and deeds, avoiding all paternalistic attitudes. We are asked to dedicate time to the poor, give them loving attention, listen to them with interest, choose them as companions … searching together how to transform their situation.… Only the closeness that makes us friends enables us to appreciate deeply the values of today's poor, their legitimate yearnings and their specific way of living the faith… The poor become subjects of evangelization and full human development.

*CELAM*

...........................

37 *Be Slow to Condemn*

...........................

Don't condemn your brother. Don't call his baseness sin, don't be quick to blame him or reject him, you who have meekness as your profession. Where it is possible show humility, put your brother before yourself, without damage to yourself, because to condemn him and despise him is the same as distancing him from Christ and from his only hope, the same as cutting the hidden wheat along with the darnel, and perhaps a wheat more precious than you. Indeed, both correct him — and this with gentleness and love, not as an enemy but like a doctor who is precise and knows where to cauterize and cut — and also be aware of yourself and your own weakness.

After all, isn't it the case that if you are suffering from cataract or some other eye condition, you don't see the sun clearly? And if you see everything swirl-

ing round because you have vertigo or are drunk,
do you blame your state on others? You need to
reflect and suffer a lot before condemning someone
of impiety.

*Gregory Nazianzen*

......................................

## 38 *Evangelizer of the Universe*

......................................

The various regions, nations, social groupings,
have each their particular apostles. And I, Lord God,
for my (very lowly) part, would wish to be the apostle
— and, if I dare say so, the evangelist — of your Christ
in the universe. I would like through meditations, the
word and the practice of my whole life to reveal and
preach the relationships of continuity that make of
the cosmos in which we move an environment divin-
ized by the Incarnation, divinizing by communion,
diminishable by our cooperation. To bring Christ, in
virtue of bonds that are truly organic, into the very
heart of realities that are considered most dangerous,
most naturalistic, most pagan — that's my Gospel
and my mission.

*Teilhard de Chardin*

.......................

## 39  *You Chose Them*

.......................

Y ou have sent me among people. Having loaded on my shoulder the weight of your powers and the strength of your grace, you told me to go. Your word that sent me far from you among those you want to save, among humanity, was hard and almost harsh.

Even before your word consecrated me for this mission I had indeed already always dealt with them. I loved to love and to be loved, to be a good friend and to have good friends. It is lovely to be that way with people and also easy because you go only to those you choose and stay as long as you choose.

But now, no. The people to whom I am sent — you choose them, not me. Nor do I have to be their friend, but rather servant. And the fact that I start getting bored is not a sign to leave, as it once was, but rather your command to stay.

*Karl Rahner*

...........................

## 40  *The "Art of Arts"*

...........................

F aced with the increasing scarcity of priests in many local churches and with the continual demand for liturgical services, priests run the risk of reducing their lives to a series of sacred functions, without establishing profound personal relationships with their neighbors.... To become a man of communion and dialogue, we must pay full attention to every single person. All are sons and daughters of God, all of them have infinite value. According to the pastoral rule of Saint Gregory the Great, who has much influenced the life of pastors throughout the centuries, "the art of arts" is the ability to lead people entrusted to our care to God. But how can we guide others, without a constant effort to establish profound relationships with them in the love and truth of Christ, without listening, to our neighbor, emptying ourselves in front of every human being.

*Toni Weber*

...........................................

## 41 *Sacraments and Radiating Love*

...........................................

The clergy has the duty of ordering and encouraging the reception of the sacraments, and this means that it tends to measure and to perceive the Christian quality of Christians simply by means of their reception of the sacraments. No one will deny that this is absolutely commanded by the Lord; but still less may one overlook the fact that the reception of the sacraments, like everything in the Church, is ordered to the life of Christian love; and the pastor should not be unaware that many people who go seldom to the sacraments … permit Christian love to shine forth more brightly than others. A parish priest in Paris, with a parish in which only a small percentage of the Christians go to Church, has laid the emphasis on first persuading the others to undertake a commitment of practical charity to those who are poorest and thus to open from within the access to the meaning of the sacraments … and the meaning of the sacraments certainly lies elsewhere than in living on one's own spiritual resources.

*Hans Urs von Balthasar*

## 42  *Becoming a Home for One Another*

A worthy person, who has found his dwelling in God, must in turn become a home for many others. We offer one another a spiritual homeland and this is a real task. To become a home for someone means for me: to be selfless. Paul speaks of the "constant influx of people." He wants to "make himself all things to everyone." If we manage in this way to give ourselves selflessly to people and offer them a spiritual homeland, then we can lead them easily also to find their homeland in God. If, however, something is lacking, then a ring on the chain is out of place. It's a question, therefore, of people becoming a home for one another.

*Joseph Kentenich*

## 43 *"Here Comes Everyone"*

The whole people of God is a holy and priestly people, because it embodies Christ's embrace of us all in our messy lives, with all their weakness and failures.... The holiness of the Church is shown in its inclusion of sinners, not their exclusion. As James Joyce said of the Church: "Here comes everyone...." I finally came to love my priesthood in the confessional box. It was here that I discovered that ordination brings us close to people just when they feel farthest away from God. We are one with them, at their sides, as together we face human frailty, failure and sin, ours and theirs. The trouble with clericalism is not that it made the priest a sacred figure, but rather its understanding of the sacred was derived from the Old Testament rather than from the gospel.

*Fr. Timothy Radcliffe, O.P.*

## 44 *Enlarge Our Heart*

We need to enlarge our heart to the measure of the heart of Jesus. How much work that means! Yet this is the only thing necessary. When this is done, all is done. It means loving everyone we meet as

God loves them. And since we live in time, we must love our neighbors one by one, without holding in our heart any left-over affection for the brother or sister met a moment before. It is the same Jesus, after all, whom we love in everyone. If anything leftover remains, it means that the preceding brother or sister was loved for our sake or for theirs … not for Jesus. That is the problem.

Our most important task is to maintain the chastity of God and this is: to keep love in our hearts as Jesus loves. Hence, to be pure we need not deprive our heart and repress the love in it. We need to enlarge our heart to the measure of the heart of Jesus and love everyone. And as one sacred host, from among the millions of hosts on the earth, is enough to nourish us with God, so one brother or sister, the one whom God's will puts next to us, is enough to give us communion with humanity, which is the mystical Jesus.

*Chiara Lubich*

# 5

# Unity among Priests

............................

45 *A Fraternal Spirit*

............................

In a fraternal spirit, priests should extend hospitality, cultivate kindliness and share their goods in common. They should be particularly solicitous for the sick, the afflicted, those overburdened with work, the lonely, those exiled from their homeland, and those who suffer persecution. They should gladly and joyfully gather together for recreation.…

And further, in order that priests may find mutual assistance in the development of their spiritual and intellectual life, that they may be able to cooperate more effectively in their ministry and be saved from the dangers of loneliness which may arise, it is necessary that some kind of common life or some sharing of common life be encouraged among priests. This, however, may take many forms, according to different personal or pastoral needs, such as living together where this is possible, or having a common table, or at least by frequent and periodic meetings.

*Second Vatican Council*

## 46 *Peace among Brothers*

Peace among brothers is the will of God
And the joy of Christ.
It is perfection in holiness,
rule of justice,
teacher of doctrine,
safeguard of customs,
praiseworthy discipline in all things.

*Saint Peter Chrysologos*

## 47 *A Question of Credibility*

Perhaps as never before, today the credibility of
the priestly ministry depends on how much priests
are themselves rooted in a lived unity, in a form of
life that enables the priestly service to be a common
witness, with the Lord himself, the One Priest, in our
midst. If a priest is to be a specialist in anything, then
he must be so in communion, in unity. The spirituality and form of life of priests is that of unity … But
such a service of unity and for unity cannot be lived
by priests in isolation. It is only by living in unity with
their bishop and in the unity of the presbyterate that
they can show that it is not they who work or speak
but the Lord.

*Klaus Hemmerle*

## 48 *Christ Is the One Who Feeds*

$G$ood pastors are all in unity, they are one. In those who feed, it is Christ who feeds. The friends of the bridegroom do not raise their own voices, they rejoice when they hear the voice of the bridegroom. When they feed the sheep it is Christ who feeds and who can therefore say, "I feed," for in them is his voice and his charity.

Let us return to Peter. In the act of entrusting his sheep to him, Christ wishes to identify with him in such a way that, in handing over the sheep to him, the Lord remains the head and Peter represents the body, the Church, and both of them, like spouses, are "two in one flesh." With this in mind, … what does he ask before handing them over? "Peter, do you love me?" And Peter replies, "Yes, I love you." And again he asks, "Do you love me?" And Peter, "Yes, I love you." And a third time, "Do you love me?" And Peter, "Yes, I love you." He confirms his love in order to seal their unity.

In pastors like this it is the one pastor who feeds, for all are in unity.

*Saint Augustine*

## 49 *This Can Be a Future for Me Too*

And it is therefore important to live in the reality of the presbyterate, of the community of priests who help one another, who are journeying on together with solidarity in their common faith. This also seems to me to be important, for if young people see priests who are very lonely, sad and tired, they will think: "If this is my future, then it is not for me." A real communion of life that shows young people: "Yes, this can be a future for me too, it is possible to live like this," must be created.

*Pope Benedict XVI*

## 50 *A Life in Common*

One cannot sufficiently recommend to priests a life lived in common and directed entirely toward their sacred ministry; the practice of having frequent meetings with a fraternal exchange of ideas, counsel and experience with their brother priests; the movement to form associations which encourage priestly holiness.

Priests should reflect on the advice of the Council, which reminds them of their common sharing in the priesthood so that they may feel a lively responsibility for fellow priests troubled by difficulties which gravely endanger the divine gift they have. They should have a burning charity for those who have greater need of love, understanding and prayer, who have need of prudent but effective help, and who have a claim on their unbounded charity as those who are, and should be, their truest friends.

*Pope Paul VI*

## 51 *The New "Family" of Priests*

How can we make demands on a priest that he leave everything: father, mother, brothers, fields ... if we do not offer him a new family, a life of communion among priests?

Jesus did not behave in this way! Of course, he asked his friends to leave everything and follow him; ... but at the same time he offered and guaranteed them a life together as a body, a new family which practiced the communion of goods and in living daily with him....

We need to allow this fraternal communion among priests to grow in a very concrete way: a communion of everything — from money to health, from the spiritual life to study and the building of bonds that are stronger, more vital and more concrete than those of a natural family. In other words, priests who live with Jesus in their midst (cf. Mt 18:20)....

From my contacts with many priests, I have felt a very strong need to help them find a home, a place where they can live together as a family. In fact, I think that if a priest does not have such a home where he can live a family life with others, eventually, he will be faced with many problems.

*Toni Weber*

....................

52 *One Presbytery*

....................

This spiritual way of life has its own ways of communion and of reciprocal fraternal contact. Jesus called his disciples personally, but not as isolated individuals. Jesus' style of life is of a communitarian kind and is the basis for life in communion.

This applies in a particular way to the life of a priest. Through priestly ordination ... we are inserted in one single presbytery. We call ourselves brothers. Priests should therefore meet together, visit one another, share their good and bad pastoral experiences, console and support one another and help one another in solidarity. There ought to be true friendships among priests.

The entry of modern bourgeois individualism into the priesthood has not been a good thing. Priestly communities in the style of *"Jesus-Caritas"* of the community of Charles de Foucauld, Schönstatt priests, or priest Focolarini can be very helpful and enriching.

*Cardinal Walter Kasper*

## 53 *The Priest: A "Trinitarian" Person*

We priests, since we are called to live the life and mission of Jesus, must be at the service of a Church increasingly modeled on the life of the Trinity....

The priest is a Trinitarian person, like Jesus, and like him he is called to proclaim and promote a new life. This is not simply the revelation of God who is one and triune, it is the communication of divine life, of an *agapic* existence that is the measure of human life together.... We priests are those that "gather together God's family as a brotherhood, all of one mind" (LG 28)....

But how can we do this without being experts, without the experience of Trinitarian communion among us, as members of the priestly Body? The same paragraph of the Council document adds, "all priests are bound together in intimate brotherhood...."

We cannot allow this "sacramental fraternity" to remain simply a nice formula that means nothing of substance in our lives.

*Jesús Castellano Cervera*

# 6

# Learning the Art of Loving

......................................................

54 *The World Belongs to Those Who Love it*

......................................................

At times we complain that Christianity in to-day's world is always more marginalized, that it has become difficult to pass on the faith to the young, and that vocations are diminishing. One could continue listing reasons for worry....

Not infrequently in fact, we feel ourselves lost in today's world, but the adventure of hope brings us beyond that. One day I found these words written on a calendar, "The world belongs to those who love it and to those who know how to prove it." How true these words are! In the heart of every person there is an infinite thirst for love, and with the love which God has placed in our hearts (cf. Rom 5:5) we can satisfy that thirst.

However, it is necessary that our love be an "art," an art that exceeds the ability to love in a merely human way. Much, if not all, depends on this art.

I have seen this art lived, for example, by Mother Teresa of Calcutta. Whoever met her loved her. Likewise, Pope John XXIII … many years after his death, his memory is still alive among the people.

*Cardinal Francis Xavier Van Thuan*

...............................

## 55 *To Tell You I Love You*

...............................

I once heard it said of a priest, that "his people knew that he loved them." It would be hard to think of a great tribute than that, not easy to find a better epitaph. He may have been a fine preacher, an excellent administrator, a good theologian, a wonderful broadcaster, admirably efficient; but what are these if there is no love?… Odd, is it not, that we rarely hear St. Paul's hymn to charity at an ordination to the priesthood, and yet it would be so very appropriate and, indeed, so practical too.… A priest has to show the face of Christ, firm in respect of principles, but always kind and loving. When the people know that you love them, then they are drawn to see something of the love of God which God has for each one — the ambassador has not only spoken about that but also shown it in his ministry.

*Basil Hume*

## 56 *With the Eyes of Christ*

Love of neighbor is thus shown to be possible in the way proclaimed by the Bible, by Jesus. It consists in the very fact that, in God and with God, I love even the person whom I do not like or even know. This can only take place on the basis of an intimate encounter with God, an encounter which has become a communion of will, even affecting my feelings. Then I learn to look on this other person not simply with my eyes and my feelings, but from the perspective of Jesus Christ.... Going beyond exterior appearances, I perceive in others an interior desire for a sign of love, of concern. This I can offer them not only through the organizations intended for such purposes, accepting it perhaps as a political necessity. Seeing with the eyes of Christ, I can give to others much more than their outward necessities; I can give them the look of love for which they crave.

*Pope Benedict XVI*

## 57 *From* Ex Opere Operato *to* Ex Opere Operantis

When we act in the Church's name in dispensing the sacraments, we are instruments of God by which grace is conferred by the simple performance of the action or, as the Scholastics said, *ex opere operato*. Sunlight is not polluted by passing through a dirty window. God can write straight with crooked lines. A person could be validly baptized by a Judas as by a Peter. This is true of the sacraments. But the priest is bound to perform many other duties — to console the sick, to preach the Gospel, to convert sinners, to stir souls to penance, to foster vocations — and all these duties require our own sacrifice, our detachment and the laborious fashioning of ourselves to the image of Christ. The effectiveness of such actions *ex opere operantis* requires the surrender of our personality to Christ…. We act, live, think and preach not in our name or personality, but in His…. Our oneness in Him is so total, that we cry out with Paul: "I hang upon the Cross, and yet I am alive; or rather, not I; it is Christ that lives in me."

*Fulton Sheen*

58 *Love Them Anyway*

People are unreasonable, illogical, and self-centered,
LOVE THEM ANYWAY
If you do good, people will accuse you of
selfish, ulterior motives,
DO GOOD ANYWAY
If you are successful,
you win false friends and true enemies,
SUCCEED ANYWAY
The good you do will be forgotten tomorrow,
DO GOOD ANYWAY
Honesty and frankness make you vulnerable,
BE HONEST AND FRANK ANYWAY
What you spent years building may be
destroyed overnight,
BUILD ANYWAY
People really need help
but may attack you if you help them,
HELP PEOPLE ANYWAY
Give the world the best you have
And you'll get kicked in the teeth,
GIVE THE WORLD THE BEST YOU'VE GOT ANYWAY.

*Mother Teresa*

## 59  *Generating Christ*

Let all things be done in charity. In this way we will be able to overcome the innumerable difficulties that we have day by day. And in this way we will have the strength to generate Christ in us and in others.

*Saint Charles Borromeo*

## 60  *The Only Thing They Need*

Oh, these creatures, my God, to whom you sent me, far away from you! Most … do not want your gifts at all, your grace, your truth, that you sent me with. And I must nevertheless go back time and time again to their door, importunate as a travelling salesman with his trinkets. If at least I only knew for sure that they want to reject you when they don't receive me, that would be some consolation.…

And those who allow me into their lives? Lord, they even want completely different things than those I bring from you.… If it is not money they seek, or material help, or the slight comfort of compassion, they see me as a kind of agent selling insurance, with which they can insure their life after death.…

Lord, teach me to pray and to love you. Then in you I will forget my misery.... And only then will I be a brother for all people, someone who helps them to find you, the only one they need, God of my brothers and sisters.

*Karl Rahner*

........................................

## 61 *Sharing of Material Goods*

........................................

The same certainty of the radicality of the presence of God in others that favors communion (interchange) between one person and another, leads to a sharing of material goods too. The communion of goods — perhaps the newest and most meaningful social phenomenon of the first Christian community — cannot be considered optional ... in order to feel good.... It is in fact the real proof ... of a personal response to the love of God and therefore to love of neighbor. This too is a way of losing in order to be: we detach ourselves from idols (mammon) in order to enter into communion. When a neighbor needs something, if I have it and do not give it, the Fathers of the Church would say that I am a murderer. To give to someone in need is to restore to God what is his.

*Silvano Cola*

## 62  *Without Love – No Preaching*

[ The Lord] sent the disciples out two by two to proclaim the Gospel because there are two precepts of charity, the love of God and love of neighbor and because charity cannot be exercised by less than two persons. Because no one, properly speaking, exercises charity towards himself. Rather love must strive towards another for it to become charity. Though without comment, the Lord sent out his disciples two by two in order also to make us divine that the ministry of preaching should not be exercised by those who do not have love for their neighbor.

*Saint Gregory the Great*

..........................................

## 63  *A Person Who Has Charity*

..........................................

A person who has charity is not proud; does not love to dominate others; can never be heard finding fault with their conduct; does not love to speak about what others are doing. A person who has charity does not question the intentions of others, does not believe he can do things better than they do; never places himself above his neighbor. On the contrary, such a person believes that others always do things better than he does. He does not take offence when a neighbor is given preference. If he is despised, he is still happy, because he thinks that he deserves even more contempt.

You see that in order to love the good God and your neighbor it's not necessary to be very erudite or rich. It's enough to try and please God in everything that we do, doing good to all, to the good and bad alike, to those who harm our reputation as to those who love us.

*Saint John Mary Vianney*

# 7

# Unifying Life

## 64 *Co-ordinating Life*

Priests, too, involved and constrained by so many obligations of their office, certainly have reason to wonder how they can coordinate and balance their interior life with feverish outward activity. Neither the mere external performance of the works of the ministry, nor the exclusive engagement in pious devotion, although very helpful, can bring about this necessary coordination. Priests can arrive at this only by following the example of Christ our Lord in their ministry. His food was to follow the will of him who had sent him to accomplish his work....

In order to measure and verify this coordination of life in a concrete way, let priests examine all their works and projects to see what is the will of God.

*Second Vatican Council*

## 65 *Organize Your Work*

There are moments and situations when urgent action and sustained effort are needed. But there are also other circumstances, many of which are wrongly deemed unavoidable, in which time is wasted to the detriment of the spiritual and interior life....

Many priests let themselves be dragged into the current of activism, claiming as duties things which are not required at all, when they could be put off or put aside, or lessened at least. In the active life it is very easy to fall prey to extremes that must be avoided at all costs. Priests must not omit prayer, in which they will always find light and in which they can find the remedy for many evils. They must put God in the first place; but to do this they must put order into their working life....

It is beautiful to give yourself without measure to others, but only after strengthening the soul with the action of the Holy Spirit and having received his purity, his strength, his light and his love.

*Conchita Cabrera De Armida*

## 66 *"Being Created" in Prayer*

Prayer finds its source in God's holiness and is at the same time our response to this holiness. I once wrote, "Prayer makes the priest and through prayer the priest becomes himself." Before all else the priest must indeed be a man of prayer, convinced that time devoted to personal encounter with God is always spent in the best way possible. This not only benefits him; it also benefits his apostolic work.

*Pope John Paul II*

## 67 *Unify Everything in the Trinity*

The priest must imitate the *Father*, for he is also a father in his most pure fruitfulness and in his love for people, with all the qualities of a father, of the Father in heaven, in whose mind he was generated.

He must imitate the *Son*, who I am, the Word made Man, transforming himself into Me. This means not merely imitating me, but being another Me on earth, in order to glorify the Father in every act of his life and to give him souls for heaven.

And he must imitate the *Holy Spirit* being love, spreading love, enabling people to fall in love with

Love. Fused in charity, permeated by love, he must spread and witness to the Word through love and unify everyone in the Trinity, which is totally love, with all the infinite consequences that flow from that.

Union: solidarity in judgments, in opinions, in decisions: unifying everything, minds and hearts, in the Trinity.

*Conchita Cabrera De Armida*

........................

## 68 *"Multiply" Time*

........................

A contemplative life means becoming aware of the presence of God in all things, allowing him to touch and move us, letting ourselves be possessed and filled by God who is present, by God in God, by God in the world, by God in the Church, and in the community. In other words, by God above us and in us, by God outside and on earth, by God in our midst, at the center. What counts is not missing any opportunity for being with him and staying close to him: being attached to the "absolute in our midst."

To remain in a contemplative state requires time. And it seems that we have no time. Yet is it not truer that time escapes us, when we reduce the time we spend in contemplation? The more things I have to do, the more I need to pray. And a kind of "miraculous increase in time" happens. Because of the time given to God, I have more time available or at least more quality time, when I am more open to others, more full of love to give to others.

*Klaus Hemmerle*

..............................

## 69 *Like in a Monastery*

..............................

When we put our hand into a basin of water,
when we stir up the fire with a bamboo stalk,
when we line up endless columns of numbers on
    a page of accounts,
when we are dried up by the sun
and sink into the mud of a rice field,
when we have to work at the smelter's furnace,
if we do not repeat exactly
the same religious life
as we would if we were at prayer in a monastery,
the world will not be saved.

*Mahatma Gandhi*

## 70 *That Uninterrupted Dialogue*

Jesus did not merely participate in public and prescribed worship services. Perhaps even more often the Gospels tell of *solitary prayer* in the still of the night, on open mountain tops, in the wilderness far from people. Jesus' public ministry was preceded by forty days and forty nights of prayer. Before he chose and commissioned his twelve apostles, he withdrew into the isolation of the mountains. By his hour on the Mount of Olives, he prepared himself for his road to Golgotha. A few short words tell us what he implored of his Father during this most difficult hour of his life, words that are given to us as guiding stars for our own hours on the Mount of Olives. "Father, if you are willing, take this cup away from me. Nevertheless, let your will be done, not mine." Like lightning, these words for an instant illumine for us the innermost spiritual life of Jesus, the unfathomable mystery of his God-man existence and his dialogue with the Father. Surely, this dialogue was life-long and uninterrupted.

*Edith Stein*

## 71 *Distracted by Too Many Things*

Often pastoral concerns keep a person busy in many things and he becomes incapable of attending to everything because the mind is taken up with so many worries. The wise man forbids this with wise words: "My son, don't involve yourself in too many things" (Sirach 11:10). When the mind is distracted by too many concerns, it cannot apply itself to specific areas of action. If worrying during activity is too much, a person no longer has the strength that comes from interior recollection. He becomes anxious in the ordering of external things, and, ignorant of himself, knows how to think of many things, but he does not know himself.

*Saint Gregory the Great*

## 72 *Imbibing a New Set of Ideas*

I say, then, it is plain to common sense that the man who has not accustomed himself to the language of heaven will be no fit inhabitant of it … The case is like that of a language or style of speaking of this world; we know well a foreigner from a native … so a habit of prayer, the practice of turning to God and the unseen world, in every season, in every place, in every emergency (let alone its supernatural effect of prevailing with God) — prayer, I say, has what may be called a natural effect, in spiritualizing and elevating the soul. A man is no longer what he was before; gradually, imperceptibly to himself he has imbibed a new set of ideas, and become imbued with fresh principles.

*John Henry Newman*

# 8

# Living Eucharistically,
# Living and Preaching the Word

....................................

73 *In Love with the Eucharist*

....................................

$B$y virtue of sacred Orders, the priest receives
the gift of and commitment to repeat in the Sacrament the gestures and words with which Jesus
instituted the memorial of his Pasch at the Last
Supper.... We are well aware that the validity of
the Sacrament does not depend on the holiness of
the celebrant, but its effectiveness for him and for
others will be all the greater the deeper the faith,
the more ardent the love and the more fervent the
spirit of prayer with which he lives it.... Thinking
of priests in love with the Eucharist, we cannot ...
forget St. John Mary Vianney, the humble parish
priest of Ars at the time of the French Revolution.
With the holiness of his life and his pastoral zeal,
he succeeded in making that little village a model
Christian community, enlivened by the Word of
God and by the sacraments.

*Pope Benedict XVI*

## 74 *Continue Your Mass*

Let those who are called to follow Jesus in priestly celibacy and to share in his priesthood, pray and ask for the courage to give — "to give until it hurts." This giving is true love in action and we can do it only when we are one with Jesus.… How completely the priest must be one with Jesus for Jesus to use him in his place, in his name, to utter his words, do his actions … You must continue your Mass after its daily celebration during the Liturgy, by your sincere fidelity to the little moment-to-moment things of life.…

*Mother Teresa*

..........................

## 75 *Directed to the Eucharist*

..........................

In the celebration of the Eucharist, the one sacrifice acceptable to God … is offered through the ministry of priests in the form of a sacrament. And so, through their ministry, the spiritual sacrifice which the faithful make of their own prayer and Christian lives is rendered complete through being joined to the one acceptable sacrifice of Christ. The entire ministry of priests is directed to this central act and therein it finds its completion. Their ministry, which begins with the preaching of the Gospel, "draws its force and power from the sacrifice of Christ and tends to this, that 'the whole redeemed city,' that is, the whole assembly and community of the saints, should be offered as a universal sacrifice to God through the High Priest who offered himself in his Passion for us that we might be the body of so great a Head" (*Presbyterorum ordinis*, 2).

*Cardinal Desmond Connell*

## 76 *The Most Beautiful Masses of My Life!*

When I was arrested, I had to leave immediately with empty hands.... The faithful … sent me a small bottle of wine for Mass with a label that read, "medicine for stomach-aches." They also sent some hosts, which they hid in a flashlight for protection against the humidity. The police asked me, "You have stomach-aches?" "Yes." "Here's some medicine for you."

I will never be able to express my great joy! Every day, with three drops of wine and a drop of water in the palm of my hand, I would celebrate Mass. This was my altar, and this was my cathedral! It was true medicine for soul and body, "Medicine of immortality, remedy so as not to die but to have life always in Jesus" as Saint Ignatius of Antioch says.

Each time I celebrated the Mass, I had the opportunity to extend my hands and nail myself to the cross with Jesus, to drink with him the bitter chalice. Each day in reciting the words of consecration, I confirmed with all my heart and soul a new pact, an eternal pact between Jesus and me through his blood mixed with mine. Those were the most beautiful masses of my life!

*Cardinal Francis Xavier Van Thuan*

..............................

## 77 *Living Eucharistically*

..............................

Saint Augustine points out that unlike ordinary food, which after ingestion we change into ourselves, the food of the Eucharist assimilates us to Christ. By eating his Body each day we gradually acquire his attitudes and sentiments: we learn to see people and events through his eyes. Consequently, if priests have a deep Eucharistic life they will easily acquire the essential priestly virtues which we see reflected in Christ's life as we read the pages of the Gospel.... Despite his human limitations the priest has a duty to try and develop those natural virtues — cheerfulness, generosity, empathy — which make his pastoral work more effective. Above all he needs to mature his talents for communication and social interaction....

*Thomas McGovern*

## CHAPTER EIGHT

## 78  To Become "Eucharist" for Others

For the greater majority, this "giving of one's life" that Jesus speaks of is not accomplished through blood. It is achieved in the many small actions of everyday life, in putting ourselves at the service of others, including those whom, for whatever reason, might seem "inferior" to us....

To serve means to become "Eucharist" for others, to identify ourselves with them, to share their joys and sorrows, to learn to think with their heads, to feel with their hearts, to live their lives "to walk in their moccasins" as an Indian proverb says.

*Cardinal Francis-Xavier Van Thuan*


## 79  Prolong the Presence of Christ

Priests are called to prolong the presence of Christ, the one high priest, embodying his way of life and making him visible in the midst of the flock entrusted to their care....

In the Church and on behalf of the Church, priests are a sacramental representation of Jesus Christ — the head and shepherd — authoritatively proclaiming his word, repeating his acts of forgiveness and his offer of salvation — particularly in baptism, penance and the Eucharist, showing his loving concern to the point of a total gift of self for the flock, which they gather into unity and lead to the Father through Christ and in the Spirit. In a word, priests exist and act in order to proclaim the Gospel to the world and to build up the Church in the name and person of Christ the head and shepherd.

*Pope John Paul II*

## 80  *"One Body, One Spirit in Christ"*

We celebrate the Eucharist rightly if with our thoughts and our being we enter into the words which the Church sets before us. There we find the prayer of all generations, which accompany us along the way towards the Lord. As priests, in the Eucharistic celebration we are those who by their prayer blaze a trail for the prayer of today's Christians. If we are inwardly united to the words of prayer, if we let ourselves be guided and transformed by them, then the faithful will also enter into those words. And then all of us will become truly "one body, one spirit" in Christ.

*Pope Benedict XVI*

## 81 Renewed by the Word

The disciples are thus drawn deep within God by being immersed in the word of God. The word of God is, so to speak, the bath which purifies them, the creative power which transforms them into God's own being. So then, how do things stand in our own lives? Are we truly pervaded by the word of God? Is that word truly the nourishment we live by, even more than bread and the things of this world? Do we really know that word? Do we love it? Are we deeply engaged with this word to the point that it really leaves a mark on our lives and shapes our thinking? Or is it rather the case that our thinking is constantly being shaped by all the things that others say and do? Aren't prevailing opinions the criterion by which we all too often measure ourselves? Do we not perhaps remain, when all is said and done, mired in the superficiality in which people today are generally caught up? Do we allow ourselves truly to be deeply purified by the word of God?

*Pope Benedict XVI*

## 82 Teachers Because They Are Witnesses

For the Church, the first means of evangelization is the witness of an authentically Christian life, given over to God in a communion that nothing should destroy and at the same time given to one's neighbor with limitless zeal.… "Modern man listens more willingly to witnesses than to teachers, and if he does listen to teachers, it is because they are witnesses."

St. Peter expressed this well when he held up the example of a reverent and chaste life that wins over even without a word those who refuse to obey the word.

It is therefore primarily by her conduct and by her life that the Church will evangelize the world, in other words, by her living witness of fidelity to the Lord Jesus — the witness of poverty and detachment, of freedom in the face of the powers of this world, in short, the witness of sanctity.

*Pope Paul VI*

## 83 Only Beauty Captures Hearts

It is not enough to deplore and denounce the ugly things of our world. Nor is it enough for our disenchanted era to speak of justice, duties, common good, pastoral programs, Gospel demands. We need to speak of all this with a heart charged with compassionate love, living the experience of the love that gives with joy and gives rise to enthusiasm. We need to radiate the beauty of what is true and just in life, because only this beauty really captures hearts and directs them to God.

*Cardinal Carlo Maria Martini*

...............................

## 84 *Antidote to Clericalism*

...............................

Clericalism is that deformation so clearly challenged by Jesus to which all "professionals" of religion are exposed. It can be seen in feeling superior or in preaching for others without really oneself living deeply, or in looking for privileges and recognitions, etc. These are all expressions of human weakness that can be found in every social environment and so it is unfortunately inevitable that they exist also in the religious world.

We don't have to be concerned about being anti-clerical or anti-secularist but rather we should make the effort to relive the life of Jesus in our own lives, striving increasingly to live what St. Paul said: "It is no longer I who live but Christ who lives in me" (Gal 2:20). This is the best antidote to clericalism.

*Pasquale Foresi*

．．．．．．．．．．．．．．．

85 *Raising Up*

．．．．．．．．．．．．．．．

We frequently see, insofar as it is possible to judge here below, that the better the life of the preacher the more abundant the fruit, no matter how lowly his style, poor his rhetoric, and plain the doctrine. For the living spirit enkindles fire. But when this spirit is wanting, the gain is small, however sublime the style and doctrine. Although it is true that good style, gestures, sublime doctrine, and well-chosen words are more moving and productive of effect when accompanied by this good spirit, yet, without it, even though delightful and pleasing to the sense and the intellect, the sermon imparts little or no devotion to the will. For the will in this case will ordinarily be left as weak and remiss as before, even though wonderful things were admirably spoken; and the sermon merely delights the sense of hearing, like a musical concert or sounding bells. But the spirit, as I said, will not leave its natural ties any more than previously, since the voice does not possess the power to raise a dead man from his sepulcher.

*Saint John of the Cross*

## 86 *Hidden Yearning*

Even in the modern secularized city, in its squares and in its streets — where disbelief and indifference seem to reign, where evil seems to prevail over good, creating the impression of a victory of Babylon over Jerusalem — one can find a hidden yearning, a germinating hope, a quiver of expectation. As can be read in the book of the prophet Amos, "The days are coming, declares the Lord God, when I shall send a famine on the country: not hunger for food, not thirst for water, but famine for hearing the word of the Lord" (8:11). The evangelizing mission of the Church wants to answer this hunger.

Even the risen Christ makes an appeal to the hesitant apostles, to go forth from their protected horizon: "Go, therefore, and make disciples of all nations ... and teach them to observe the commands I gave you" (Mt 28:19–20). The Bible is fraught with appeals "not to be silent," to "speak out," to "proclaim the word at the right and at the wrong time," to be the sentinels that tear away the silence of indifference.

*2008 Synod Message on the Word of God*

······················································

## 87 *With the Same Impetus as the Beginnings*

······················································

To nourish ourselves with the word in order to be "servants of the word" in the work of evangelization: this is surely a priority for the Church at the dawn of the new millennium. Even in countries evangelized many centuries ago, the reality of a "Christian society" which, amid all the frailties which have always marked human life, measured itself explicitly on Gospel values, is now gone. Today we must courageously face a situation which is becoming increasingly diversified and demanding, in the context of "globalization" and of the consequent new and uncertain mingling of peoples and cultures. Over the years, I have often repeated the summons to the new evangelization. I do so again now, especially in order to insist that we must rekindle in ourselves the impetus of the beginnings and allow ourselves to be filled with the ardor of the apostolic preaching which followed Pentecost. We must revive in ourselves the burning conviction of Paul, who cried out: "Woe to me if I do not preach the Gospel" (1 Cor 9:16).

*Pope John Paul II*

84

# 9

# Radiating the Risen Christ, Embracing Jesus Forsaken

......................................

## 88 *The Way of Transformation*

......................................

It seems to me that in the Church's history, these questions that truly torment us are constantly cropping up in various forms: what should we do? People seem to have no need of us, everything we do seems pointless.

I therefore share with you these questions, these queries. I also suffer. However, let us, on the one hand, suffer all together for these problems, and let us also suffer in transforming the problems; for suffering itself is the way to transformation, and without suffering nothing is transformed.

This is also what the Parable of the Grain of Wheat that fell into the earth means: only in a process of suffering transformation does the fruit mature and the solution become clear....

We must take these difficulties of our time to heart and transform them, suffering with Christ, and thereby transform ourselves. And to the extent to which we ourselves are transformed, we will also be able to respond to the question asked above, we will also be able to see the presence of the Kingdom of God and to make others see it.

*Pope Benedict XVI*

..................................

## 89 *Suffering Brings Wisdom*

..................................

Those who live close to Christ impart Christ. As Saint Augustine said, "What I live by, I impart." Suffering brings wisdom, but books bring only natural understanding. The priest who has been crucified and has endured his passion with patience will always be found to be the merciful priest.… No priest sees problems so sympathetically as the priest who is standing on the watchtower of Calvary. Like the sun, it cannot be seen, and yet it illumines all else.

*Fulton Sheen*

.....................

## 90 *I Am Ashamed*

.....................

It is a great suffering … for the Church in general, for me personally, that this (crisis of priests and sexual abuse) could happen. If I read the history of these events, it is difficult for me to understand how it was possible for priests to fail in this way in the mission to give healing, to give God's love to these children. I am ashamed and we will do everything possible to ensure that this does not happen in future. I think we have to act on three levels: the first is at the level of justice and the political level. I will not speak at this moment about homosexuality: this is another thing. We will absolutely exclude pedophiles from the sacred ministry; it is absolutely incompatible, and whoever is really guilty of being a pedophile cannot be a priest. So at this first level we can do justice and help the victims, because they are deeply affected; these are the two sides of justice: one, that pedophiles cannot be priests and the other, to help in any possible way the victims. Then there is a pastoral level. The victims will need healing and help and assistance and reconciliation.… I know that the Bishops and directors of seminarians will do all possible to have a strong discernment because it is more important to have good priests than to have many priests. This is also our third level, and we hope that we can do, and have done and will do in the future, all that is possible to heal these wounds.

*Pope Benedict XVI*

## 91 *My Most Beautiful Cathedral*

During my voyage toward North Vietnam, I was put in chains three times with a man who was non-Catholic, a member of the parliament, and someone known for his fundamentalist Buddhism. Yet, being together in the same terrible situation touched his heart ... we became friends. On the ship and afterward in the re-education camp, I had occasion to dialogue with the most varied people: ministers, members of parliament, high civil and military figures.... In the camp, I was elected bursar, which gave me the responsibility of serving everyone, distributing the food, getting the hot water, and carrying on my back the coal to keep us warm during the night. All this because the other prisoners considered me a man worthy of trust.

Upon my departure from Saigon, Jesus, crucified outside the walls of Jerusalem, made me understand that I had to engage in a new form of evangelization. I no longer acted as a bishop within a diocese, but extra muros; as a missionary ad extra ... going outside....

In the obscurity of faith, in service and in humiliation, the light of hope had changed my vision. I understood that at this point, on this ship, in this prison, was my most beautiful cathedral.

*Cardinal Francis Xavier Van Thuan*

88

What is required more than ever in today's world is authenticity. It is no longer sufficient for men to simply be ordained priests. We need priests-Christ, priests-victims for humanity. Authentic Christs, always ready to die for everyone.

If this is the measure of love in the priest's life, he will have no fear of wasting time, he will not worry about having to change his job.

He will see the part of the Church entrusted to him become a garden. It will contain darnel, certainly, and hate, but also fruitful love whose effects will not cease at the edge of his territory, but go beyond.

Like at Ars, yes, like at Ars, where, after God, the curate was everything for his people, and they came from far away to breathe the odor of Christ, in order to feed themselves on him, and to live.

Let's say it, let's say it out loud: in order to live!

For without Christ, without priests-Christ, the world today, with its marvelous and extraordinary discoveries does not live. It is dying, and will die.

Christ alone is life.

*Chiara Lubich*

## 93 *The Summit of the Priesthood*

Priests are often involved in many activities, but when they realize that they spend 100% to produce 1%, they feel discouragement. Stress and doubts arise. Have I made a mistake about my vocation? Does celibacy really have any value? Why is having a family something denied to a priest?…

I had all these thoughts when the government barred me from all my activities in the Church, and I cleaned shop windows for ten years on the streets of Prague. I was forced by my situation to find my priestly identity — without my ministry, without any apparent purpose, without being a leader.

Jesus too, while he was nailed to the cross, could not work miracles, could not preach, but — abandoned — could only remain silent and suffer, reaching the summit of his priesthood. I found in him my true priestly identity, which filled me with joy and peace.

Then I understood that this identity is not acquired for all time in a moment of illumination and grace; it must be continually sought for, above all in dark and painful moments.

*Cardinal Miloslav Vlk*

And there are so many kinds of desert. There is the desert of poverty, the desert of hunger and thirst, the desert of abandonment, of loneliness, of destroyed love. There is the desert of God's darkness, the emptiness of people no longer aware of their dignity or the goal of human life. The external deserts in the world are growing, because the internal deserts have become so vast. Therefore the earth's treasures no longer serve to build God's garden for all to live in, but they have been made to serve the powers of exploitation and destruction. The Church as a whole and all her Pastors, like Christ, must set out to lead people out of the desert, towards the place of life, towards friendship with the Son of God, towards the One who gives us life, and life in abundance.

*Pope Benedict XVI*

## 95 Re-considering Confession

It is only by starting from the heart of the Gospel that the sacrament of confession can be renewed. In this way a lot of the ballast that has been dragged along throughout the centuries and that has ruined confession for many Christians will fall away. Not only the lay faithful but priests too must relate in a new way to the sacrament in order to be ready for this purpose. They too need a profound re-education and a new re-consideration of sin, confession and absolution. They too need to be helped in the new life that takes its measures from the pure spirit of Christ. And they have the task of presenting to the Christian people in preaching and catechesis a totally new awareness of the relevance of the Redemption in this central sacrament.

*Hans Urs von Balthasar*

## 96 The Shepherd and the Hireling

When comparing a true shepherd and a hireling, the difference may be seen more clearly in difficult situations. At quiet moments, in fact, a hireling behaves more or less the same way as a true shepherd. But when the wolf arrives, it is clear how each one cares for the flock.

The wolf attacks the flock when an unjust tyrant oppresses the faithful and the humble. The one who appears to be a shepherd, while he is not, abandons the sheep and flees, fearing for his own safety, and makes no attempt to combat injustice. He flees not only by going somewhere else, but also by depriving the flock of support. He flees, because he sees injustice and remains silent. He flees, because he hides himself in silence....

To put up a defense means to oppose with a free voice any powerful person who acts wrongly. We go into battle for the house of Israel ... and erect a wall, if with the authority of justice we protect the innocent faithful against the injustice of the perverse. The hireling does not do this, he flees when he sees the wolf.

*Saint Gregory the Great*

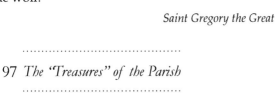

## 97 *The "Treasures" of the Parish*

Every parish has its treasures. The real treasures are the poor, those in difficulty, those suffering, the sick and all those into whom the Holy Spirit has poured out his gifts so generously that they live a life of suffering and prayer....

Every good pastor must know how to esteem and make pastoral use of these "treasures" for his ministry and for the salvation of those entrusted to him.

I would like to focus particularly on the sick. Every parish has its sick. There are the chronically ill who are being consumed gradually like a candle, awaiting, crucified on their beds, the final hour of their life. There are also those who are ill occasionally for a period of time.

Following the example of Jesus Christ the Teacher who loved particularly the poor and the sick, the priest must reserve his preferences for these children of his: "I was sick and you visited me."

*Giacomo Alberione*

## 98 *Jesus Is Mirrored in Them*

The saints are like many small mirrors in which Jesus Christ contemplates himself.

In his apostles (Jesus) contemplates his zeal and his love for the salvation of souls; in the martyrs he contemplates his patience, his sufferings and his painful death; in the solitary he sees his dark and hidden life; in virgins, he admires the purity without stain, and in all the saints, his limitless charity so that, in admiring the virtues of the saints, we do nothing other than admire the virtues of Jesus Christ.

Saints did not all start well, but all finished well.

*Saint John Mary Vianney*

## 99 If You Love, You Are

What seems to me important is that you approach priesthood with the desire to be able to die for everyone, to die to oneself for everyone. Douse every flame of knowledge or heroism and just be love. God is love. If you love, you are. If you do not love, you are not.

You must consider the other, whoever they are, as irreplaceable, unique in the world....

How many times have we read in St. Paul that even if I have the gift of prophecy and give away all I have, without charity I am nothing. The whole Gospel is there. "Whatever you did to the least, you did it to me." Whatever I do to the biggest scoundrel in the world, I do it to Jesus. This is how we can bring light into the dark night....

If you become convinced of this, it is *the* big discovery. You understand that at last the world could be better.

*Silvano Cola*

......................

## 100 *A Daily Battle*

......................

$S$ometimes it happens that the limits and defects of others make it difficult to carry out this holy obligation to recognize the figure of Jesus in them. In a deceptive way, this can lead us to give up our interest in them and so feel things are fine and that in these cases the commitment to love is lessened or has ceased. We need to know how to forgive as Jesus forgave. From the example of the Teacher we learn that there are no excuses or extenuating circumstances for not loving as Christ wants us to love or better as he himself has loved us. The capacity of seeing the good side of others is the best antidote against the pernicious tendencies that tend to highlight the negative and slanderous, so common in society. We have a battle on our hands to be fought every day in our daily relationships with our brothers and sisters.

*Cardinal Claudio Hummes*

........................

## 101 *Becoming Human*

........................

$A$s I follow Jesus Christ who humbled himself to share in our humanity, I am called to be more human and to promote whatever is good for health of body, mind and spirit in myself and in others. Thomas Merton ... used to tell his novices that to become saints they must first become men. In my journey to becoming human, I need continual patience with the workings of my body, in its interaction with my mind and spirit. As I learn more about my chemistry, my genes, my hormones and my flowing adrenalin, I can see why, in programs for priestly formation today, there is so much emphasis on human formation.... In my own fragility and in my identifying with human weakness, I manifest the broken but beautiful face of Christ.

*Tom Lane*

..............................

102 *Weakness and Strength*

..............................

A Christian's asceticism requires strength which is found in the Creator. We are darkness and he is radiant light. We are infirmity and he is robust good health. We are poverty and he is infinite wealth. We are weakness and he sustains us, "for you are, O God, my strength."

Nothing on earth is capable of stemming the impatient gushing forth of the redeeming blood of Christ. Yet human limitations can veil our eyes so that we do not notice the grandeur of God.

Hence the responsibility of all the faithful, especially those who have the role of governing — serving — the People of God spiritually, of not blocking the sources of grace, of not being ashamed of Christ's Cross.

*Saint Josemaría Escrivá De Balaguer*

..........................

## 103 *Flawed but Noble*

..........................

"Three times I begged the Lord about this, that it might leave me" (2 Cor 12:8). I have spent the last 19 years working directly with priests whose human flaws have brought them to their knees. These priests, like all of us, are flawed but noble; they have feet of clay but hearts of gold. Even in their most flawed states, there is something different about these men.... One of our long-standing psychotherapists, who was not Catholic, retired after working for many years in our program. She personally worked directly with some of the most wounded of our men. After she retired, word came back to us she had converted to Catholicism. Perhaps even in our most wounded and vulnerable state as priests, the Gospel is being preached. Perhaps it is only in such a state that Jesus is truly proclaimed.

*Stephen Rossetti*

Only through the radicality of sacrifice can we be witnesses of hope inspired, as John Paul II writes, "by Christ's own charity, which takes the form of concern, tenderness, compassion, openness, availability, and interest in people's problems" (*Redemptoris Missio*, n. 89).... In his solidarity with the least, those furthest away, those without God, Jesus Crucified opened the apostolic way of "becoming all to all." Paul, in his turn, communicates to Christians their true apostolate: to reveal to every person, without discrimination, that God is close to them and loves them infinitely.

Making ourselves "one" with everyone, and having the courage to regard every human person — including those who seem most contemptible or hostile — as "neighbor," as brother or sister, we practice the central content of salvation. We live the joyful announcement that in the cross of Jesus, God comes close to every person who is far from God, to offer pardon and redemption.

*Cardinal Francis Xavier Van Thuan*

That a good man may have his back to the wall is no more than we knew already; but that God could have his back to the wall is a boast for all insurgents for ever. Christianity is the only religion on earth that has felt that omnipotence made God incomplete.... Alone of all creeds, Christianity has added courage to the virtues of the Creator. For the only courage worth calling courage must necessarily mean that the soul passes a breaking point — and does not break.... In a garden Satan tempted man: and in a garden God tempted God.... When the world shook and the sun was wiped out of heaven, it was not at the crucifixion, but at the cry from the cross: the cry which confessed that God was forsaken of God. And now ... let the atheists themselves choose a god. They will find only one divinity who ever uttered their isolation; only one religion in which God seemed for an instant to be an atheist.

*G. K. Chesterton*

The People of God is called to go with Jesus Forsaken "outside the gate," outside the sacred camp (cf. Heb 13:12–13) to encounter the whole of humanity especially where it lives most in darkness, anguish and distance from God. In this way it unleashes the Spirit of the Risen Christ.

We might ask ourselves: What does the Church encounter outside the sacred camp? The response is surprising — thanks to Jesus' abandonment, in all that speaks of suffering and separation from God the Church finds not simply emptiness and sin but Christ himself who, as Vatican II put it, "has united himself in some way to every human being...." Wherever the People of God is to be found, the abandoned Spouse has already preceded it. Thomas Aquinas writes that Christ is the "head of all humanity" though "according to different degrees" (S. Th. III, q. 8, a. 3 c.). The key to understanding this statement is the universal embrace of the Crucified Christ. He has made all human reality his own. Like the Bride in the Song of Songs, the Church therefore is called to seek him out and discover him everywhere, and in this way to ensure the Forsaken Christ is no longer abandoned but rather unleashing his Spirit and being made manifest as Risen, the new Man who recapitulates all of humanity and the entire cosmos in himself (cf. Eph 1:10).

*Hubertus Blaumeiser*

..............................

## 107 *Disarming Ourselves*

..............................

I have waged this war against myself for many years.
It was terrible.
But now I am disarmed.
I am no longer frightened of anything
because love banishes fear.
I am disarmed of the need to be right
and to justify myself by disqualifying others.
I am no longer on the defensive holding on to my riches.
I just want to welcome and to share.
I don't hold onto my ideas and projects.
If someone shows me something better —
No, I shouldn't say better, but good —
I accept them without any regrets.
I no longer seek to compare.
What is good, true and real is always for me the best.
That is why I have no fear.

*"I Am Disarmed," by Athenagoras*
*and translated by Jean Vanier*

## 108 *A Priest's Decalogue*

1. It is more important how I live as a priest, than what I do as a priest.
2. It is more important what Christ does through me, than what I do.
3. It is more important that I live unity in the presbytery, than to throw myself headlong into ministry.
4. Service in prayer and the Word is more important than serving at tables.
5. It is more important to care spiritually for my co-workers, than to do as many activities as possible on my own.
6. It is more important to be present in a few central operative sectors, with a presence that radiates life, than being in a hurry and half-present everywhere.
7. It is more important to act in unity with your co-workers, than alone, however able you feel you are; in other words *communio* is more important than *actio*.
8. The cross is more important, because it is more fruitful, than apparent fruits that are the result of human gifts and efforts.
9. It is more important to have an openness to everything (community, diocese, universal Church), than to concentrate on particular interests, however important they seem to me.
10. It is more important that the faith is witnessed before everyone than to satisfy all the usual expectations.

*Klaus Hemmerle*

# 10

# Taking Mary into Your Home

109 *The Marian Principle in the Church*

The importance of the Marian principle in the Church was particularly highlighted after the Council ... Everything in the Church, every institution and ministry, including that of Peter and his Successors, is "included" under the Virgin's mantle, within the grace-filled horizon of her "yes" to God's will.... The two dimensions of the Church, Marian and Petrine, come together in the supreme value of *charity*, which constitutes the fulfillment of each.... Everything in this world will pass away. In eternity only Love will remain....

Indeed, the first thing that Mary did after receiving the Angel's message was to go "in haste" to the house of her cousin Elizabeth in order to be of service to her (cf. Lk 1: 39). The Virgin's initiative was one of genuine charity; it was humble and courageous, motivated by faith in God's Word and the inner promptings of the Holy Spirit. Those who love forget about themselves and place themselves at the service of their neighbor. Here we have the image and model of the Church!

*Pope Benedict XVI*

......................................

110 *Taking Mary into Your Home*

......................................

While Jesus was dying he turned to his mother, and indicating John, said, "Woman, behold your son" (Jn 19:26). Then looking at John he added, "Behold your mother." (Jn 1:27). At that moment, in John, Jesus was entrusting Mary to every Christian. But we cannot overlook the fact that John was a priest. Therefore, on that day, in the person of John, priests received from Jesus an invitation and a command: to consider Mary as their mother, and to take her home with them....

Mary is at home with priests. Priests should remember that. But even if sadly they might forget to take Mary with them, the mother of Jesus will never forget, throughout the centuries, to carry out the wishes of her dying son. Mary is the best help that Jesus has given to priests in their service to the Church.

*Chiara Lubich*

## 111  *Mary — the Pre-history of Christ Who Comes*

Mary is the woman through whom the Lord came into this world. Conceiving as a virgin out of obedience, receiving the Son of God as a gift to then lose him and, with empty hands, simply wait for Pentecost — that was her journey. The Church is in her, all of us are in her. In her is the life of those called by Christ and gathered by him; in her too there's the vocation to the perfection of love in the "imperfection" of the form of life; the calling to pure totality that is to be found in pure provisionality and in pure emptiness. Mary is and remains the pre-history of Christ who comes. All those who are called to witness with their life to the Christ who comes, find themselves in her.

*Klaus Hemmerle*

## 112  *The Water for Today*

We are today in the desert of the world, the desert of morality, the desert of meaning.... God appears to be saying to each one of us, as he said to Aaron and Moses, "Can water come out of this rock?"

We are that rock, that heart of stone that God wants to change into a heart of flesh. God says to each one of us: can water, that is Jesus, come out of this rock? And we must reply: I am certain that water will come from this rock.

Faith is required. The faith that Mary had is the absolute silence of a created being that does not seek any explanations. Faith that is "absolute silence." Do you believe? I believe.

This, however, is what God is asking us collectively in the desert of humanity today. From this rock, from this heart of stone of humanity, can water, life, flow out? Can Jesus satisfy the thirst of humanity?

Yes, because all of us together, by living Mary, can generate Christ in the midst of humanity in a mystical way. This is the water that we must give to humanity.

*Silvano Cola*

..................................

113 *Wholly Effective Presence*

..................................

Without Mariology Christianity threatens imperceptibly to become inhuman. The Church becomes functionalistic, soulless, a hectic enterprise without any point of rest, estranged from her true nature by the planners. And because, in this manly-masculine world, all that we have is one ideology replacing another, everything becomes polemical, critical, bitter, humorless, and ultimately boring, and people in their masses run away from such a Church.... (Mary) can show the apostles and their successors how one can be both wholly effective presence and wholly extinguished service. For the Church was already present in her before men were set in office.

*Hans Urs von Balthasar*

## 114 *Knowing How to "Lose"*

Is it really possible for us to "lose" ourselves again and again in order to reach out to those of other cultures, particularly those in our own society who have partly or entirely renounced their Christian background? Well, there is one human being who did that so completely that she even won us over! Since the Annunciation, it could be said that (Mary) belonged in a special way to the Trinitarian culture, with a deep inner relation to the Father, the Holy Spirit, and her Son. Yet, more than anyone, she went "outside the camp" and shared in her Son's annihilation.... With him, she too underwent a double exodus: by "losing" being mother of the Messiah, she lost her human role as Flower of Israel. But also, in consenting to "lose" her motherhood of God, she shared her Son's awful experience of "exodus" from the Trinity, and through that loss became Mother of all humanity. So she can help us to live the Why of the human quest intersecting with the Why of the divine search, that alone fulfils the human spirit. And, by being ready to lose all that's most human and most divine for the sake of the other, she encourages us to expand our quest to the entire human family.

*Brendan Purcell*

. . . . . . . . . . . . . . . . . . . . . . . . . . . . . . . . . . . . . . . . . . . . . . . . .

**115** *I Want to See Myself Again in You*

. . . . . . . . . . . . . . . . . . . . . . . . . . . . . . . . . . . . . . . . . . . . . . . . .

I went into church one day,
and with my heart full of trust, I asked:
"Why did you wish to remain on earth,
on every point of the earth,
in the most sweet Eucharist,
and you, you who are God,
have not found
also a way to bring here and to leave here
Mary, the mother of all of us who journey?"
In the silence he seemed to reply:
"I have not left her because I want to see her again
    in you.
Even if you are not immaculate, my love will
    virginize you,
and you, all of you,
will open your arms and hearts as mothers of
    humanity,

which, as in times past, thirsts for God
and for his mother.
It is you who now must soothe pains, soothe
  wounds,
dry tears.
Sing her litanies
and strive to mirror yourself in them."

*Chiara Lubich*

..................

## 116 *"Hail Mary"*

..................

The starvation cell did not decree the defeat of God, it became instead a tabernacle. It was as if God, coming in stealthily through the humble heart of a Franciscan, had visited "hell." Father Maximilian's presence in the bunker was necessary for the others. He managed to communicate peace and they joined him in praying out loud. They had the impression of being in church.

The prisoners died one by one until only four were left, including Father Kolbe, who was still conscious. The SS sent someone to inject him with carbolic acid.

An eyewitness relates, "I saw Father Kolbe, praying, offering them his arm.… As soon as the SS men had left, I went in. The other bodies were on the floor, with suffering written on their faces. Father Kolbe was sitting. His body was clean and luminous. His

eyes were open, his face was pure, serene, radiant.
While offering his arm, Kolbe had said "Hail, Mary!"
Those were his last words."

*From an eyewitness account,*
*reported by Enrico Pepe*

..............................................

## 117 *Mary, Woman of the Third Day*

..............................................

Hail Mary, woman of the third day, give us the
certainty that, despite everything, death will not win
out over us, that the days of injustice are numbered,
that the blaze of war is being reduced to twilight,
that the suffering of the poor is reaching its last
gasp, that hunger, racism, and drugs are becoming a
carryover from old bankruptcies, that boredom, soli-
tude and disease are the arrears of old management,
and that finally, the tears of the victims of violence
and suffering will soon be dried up like frost in the
springtime sun.

*Fr. Tonino Bello*

# 11
# Listening to the Voice of the Spirit

## 118 *Receiving with Thanksgiving*

. . . . . . . . . . . . . . . . . . . . . . . . . . . . . . . . . . .

It is not only through the sacraments and the ministries of the Church that the Holy Spirit sanctifies and leads the people of God and enriches it with virtues, but, "allotting his gifts to everyone according as he wills, he distributes special graces among the faithful of every rank. By these gifts he makes them fit and ready to undertake the various tasks and offices which contribute toward the renewal and building up of the Church.... These charisms, whether they be the more outstanding or the more simple and widely diffused, are to be received with thanksgiving and consolation for they are perfectly suited to and useful for the needs of the Church.

*Lumen Gentium*

## 119 *Many Kinds of Service*

Ministry is for each baptized person; it is charismatically given in a universality and particularity, and it should not disturb a ministerial harmony in the community — these three characteristics have the greatest practical import. Paul says often that the Spirit has given ministry to all and that services are of many kinds. Each time Paul reflects upon the diversity of functions in the Church he recalls the origin and end of this diversity, a diversity willed by God and the special work of the Holy Spirit (1 Cor 12:4f.; Rom 12:6). The diversity lives within the Church (1 Cor 12:28) with the goal of constructing it. The letters to the churches in the first century were addressed not to individuals but to communities. When individual ministers are mentioned, it was within the context of the greater life of the local community.

*Thomas O'Meara*

## 120 *The Holy Spirit*

Without the Spirit, God is far away, Christ remains in the past, the Gospel is a dead letter, the Church is a simple organization, authority a domi-

nation, mission a propaganda, worship mere evoca-
tion, and Christian action a slave morality. But in the
Spirit … the Risen Christ is present, the Gospel is the
power of life, the Church signifies Trinitarian communion, authority is a liberating service, mission is a
Pentecost, the liturgy is memorial and anticipation,
human activity is deified.

*Orthodox Patriarch Athenagoras*

...............................

## 121 *The Gift of the Spirit*

...............................

Simeon the New Theologian wrote, "the Son is
the gate … the key to the gate is the Holy Spirit.…
the home is the Father." Through the gift of the Spirit
we find our definitive dwelling with Christ in the
bosom of the Father. Just as the Father is Jesus' paradise, so, for us, thanks to the gift of the Spirit, to live
directed in the bosom of the Father by carrying out
his will becomes already on earth our Paradise. But
for this to come about we need to live every moment
what St. Paul calls the crucifixion of our "old self."
Only in this way can we share in the resurrection
of Christ having the gift of the Spirit in us that then
overflows in us in words and actions in a continuous
"Abbà, Father," directed towards the Father.

*Piero Coda*

## 122 *What the Spirit Says*

Contemplation can never be anything other than a continually new listening to "what the Spirit says to the churches" and what he unfolds from within the Church's distinctive spirit of faith.... Intimacy with the Holy Spirit of truth thus cancels out the spectator's uninvolved objectivity, with its external, critical attitude to the truth, and replaces it with an attitude which one can only describe as prayer. This prayer is total; it encompasses our beholding and our readiness to be beheld, our receiving and self-giving, our contemplating and our self-communication, in a single, undivided whole.

*Hans Urs von Balthasar*

## 123 Veni, Sancte Spiritus

Come, Holy Spirit,
And send out from heaven
Your radiant light.

Come, father of the poor,
Come, giver of gifts,
Come, light of our hearts.

Best consoler,
Sweet guest of the soul,
Sweetness of cool refreshment.

Rest in labor,
Relief in heat,
Consolation in weeping.

O most blessed light,
Fill the center of the hearts
Of your faithful.

Without your divine power,
There is nothing in humans,
Nothing is innocent.

Wash what is soiled,
Water what is dry,
Heal what is wounded.

Bend what is rigid,
Warm what is chilled,
Guide what is astray.

Give to your faithful,
Who trust in you,
The seven sacred gifts.

Give the reward of virtue,
Give the goal of salvation,
Give eternal joy.

# Sources

1. Benedict XVI, *Deus Caritas Est*, 1.
2. John Paul II, *Gift and Mystery*, Random House, New York 1996, p. 72.
3. Pasquale Foresi, *God among Men*, New City, London 1974, pp. 72, 78.
4. San Giovanni Maria Vianney, *Primavera nell'anima. 100 pagine del Curato d'Ars*, Città Nuova, Rome 2006, p. 34.
5. Teresa of Calcutta, *For Love Alone*, St. Pauls, Middlegreen, UK and Maynooth, Ireland 1993, pp. 211–212.
6. Chiara Lubich, *Essential Writings*, New City Press, New York 2007 p. 121.
7. Karl Rahner, *Meditations on Priestly Life*, Sheed & Ward, London 1973, p. 89.
8. Card. Francis Xavier Van Thuan, *Testimony of Hope* (© Daughters of St. Paul. Used by permission of Pauline Books & Media, 50 St. Paul's Avenue, Boston, MA 02130. All rights reserved), pp. 42-43.
9. See http://www.crossroadsiniciative.com/libraryarticle/212/Prayer_of _Abandonment__Charles_de_Foucauld.html.
10. Pope Benedict XVI, Chrism Mass, 20 March 2008.
11. Chiara Lubich, "Il celibato sacerdotale," *Città Nuova* 14 (1970/3) p. 9.
12. Silvano Cola, "The Evangelical Counsels," *Being One* 18 (2009/3), p. 15.
13. Pope John Paul II, Letter to Priests, Holy Thursday 1987, nn. 11–12.
14. Pasquale Foresi, *Problematica d'oggi nella Chiesa*, Città Nuova, Rome 1970, pp. 94–95.
15. Card. Stefano Kim, *Fede e amore del card. Kim Sou Hwan/2* Diary, October 24, 1984, Seoul 1997, p. 289.
16. From *Story of a Soul*, translated by John Clarke, O.C.D. ©1975, 1976, 1996 by Washington Province of Discalced Carmelites, ICS Publications, 2131 Lincoln Rd., N.E., Washington, DC 20002-1199 U.S.A. www.icspublications.org.
17. Pope Benedict XVI, Chrism Mass, 9 April 2009.
18. John Paul II, *Novo Millennio Ineunte*.
19. Tom Norris (quoting Jesus Castellano), *The Trinity, Life of God, Hope for Humanity*, New City Press, New York 2009, p. 13.
20. John Paul II, *Novo Millennio Ineunte*, 43.
21. Vatican II, *Lumen Gentium*, 10.
22. Avery Dulles, *The Priestly Office*, Paulist Press, New York 1997, p. 11.
23. John Paul II, *Christifideles Laici*, 55.
24. Richard R. Gaillardetz, in Susan Woods ed., *Ordering the Baptismal Priesthood*, Liturgical Press, Collegeville 2003, p. 39.
25. John Paul II, *Pastores Dabo Vobis*, 12.
26. John Paul II, *Novo Millennio Ineunte*, 43
27. Pope Benedict XVI, Pastoral Convention of the Diocese of Rome 26 May 2009.
28. Vatican II, *Presbyterorum Ordinis*, 9.
29. Silvano Cola, *Scritti e testimonianze*, Grottaferrata 2007, pp. 58–59.
30. Diarmuid Martin, Archbishop of Dublin, "The Parish: A New Mission Field," Melbourne July 11, 2007.

31. Luigi Giussani, *Parole ai preti*, SEI, Turin 1996, pp. 70–71.

32. Albert Vanhoye, *Old Testament Priests and the New Priest*, Petersham, MA, St. Bede's Publications, 1986, p. 317.

33. Dom Helder Camara, *Roma, due del mattino. Lettere dal Concilio Vaticano II*, San Paolo, Cinisello Balsamo 2008, p. 135.

34. Chiara Lubich, *Essential Writings*, New City Press, New York 2007, pp. 79–80.

35. Igino Giordani, *Cattolicità*, Morcelliana, Brescia 1938, pp. 215–216.

36. CELAM, Aparecida, Brazil 2007, *Final Document*, nn. 395–398.

37. Gregory Nazianzen, *Discourse on Moderation in Disputing 29*, from *La Teologia dei Padri*, vol. 4, Rome 1975, p. 126.

38. Teilhard de Chardin, *Il sacerdote*, Queriniana, Brescia 1991, pp. 36–37.

39. Karl Rahner, *Tu sei il silenzio*, Queriniana, Brescia 1969, p. 63.

40. Toni Weber, *A Priest Needs a Home*, New City, Manila 1995, pp. 45–46.

41. Hans Urs von Balthasar, *Explorations in Theology II: Sponsa Verbi*, Ignatius Press, San Francisco 1991, p. 414.

42. Josef Kentenich, in P. Wolf (ed.), *Berufen — geweiht — gesandt*, Schönstatt, Vallendar-Schönstatt 2009, p. 91.

43. Fr. Timothy Radcliffe O.P., Lecture Delivered at the National Conference of Priests, Digby Stuart College, Morehampton 3 September 2003.

44. Chiara Lubich, *Essential Writings*, New City Press, New York 2007, p. 81.

45. Vatican II, *Presbyterorum Ordinis*, 8.

46. Saint Peter Chrysologos, *Discorso*, 53; PL 52, 347.

47. Klaus Hemmerle, *"Il sacerdote oggi" Gen's* 12 (1982/6) p. 12.

48. Saint Augustine, *The Shepherds* (Ez 34: 1–16), Discourse 46, Rome 1993, pp. 161–162.

49. Benedict XVI, To the Priests of the Diocese of Aosta (Italy), 25 July 2005.

50. Paul VI, *Sacerdotalis Caelibatus*, 80–81.

51. Toni Weber, *A Priest Needs a Home*, New City, Manila 1995, pp. 40–41.

52. Card. Walter Kasper, *Servitori della gioia. Esistenza sacerdotale — Servizio Sacerdotale*, Queriniana, Brescia 2007, pp. 85–86.

53. Jesús Castellano Cervera, *"El sacerdote, hombre trinitario," La Revista Católica*, Santiago, Cile n. 1128 (2000), pp. 401–417, at pp. 403, 413, 417.

54. Card. Francis Xavier Van Thuan, *Testimony of Hope* (© Daughters of St. Paul. Used by permission of Pauline Books & Media, 50 St. Paul's Avenue, Boston, MA 02130. All rights reserved), pp. 67–68.

55. Basil Hume, *Light in the Lord*, St. Paul Publications, Middlegreen, Slough, UK 1991, pp. 78–79.

56. Pope Benedict XVI, *Deus Caritas Est*, 18.

57. Fulton Sheen, *The Priest Is Not His Own*, Ignatius Press, San Francisco 2004, pp. 54–55.

58. Taken from a sign on the wall of Shishu Bhavan, the children's home in Calcutta. See Lucinda Vardey, in *Mother Teresa: A Simple Path*, Ballantine Books, New York 1995, p. 185.

59. Saint Charles Borromeo, *Acta Ecclesiae Mediolanensis*, Milan 1599, p. 1178.

60. Karl Rahner, *Tu sei il silenzio*, Queriniana, Brescia 1969, pp. 63–64, 69.

61. Silvano Cola, "The Relevancy of a Communitarian Spirituality for Formation," *Being One* 18 (2009/3), pp. 45–49, at p. 48.

62. Saint Gregory the Great, *Homily XVII on Luke's Gospel, Sources Chrétiennes*, 485, pp. 364–365.

63. San Giovanni Maria Vianney, *Scritti scelti*, Città Nuova, Rome 1975, p. 117.
64. Second Vatican Council, *Presbyterorum Ordinis*, 14.
65. Conchita Cabrera De Armida, *Sacerdoti di Cristo*, Città Nuova, Rome 2008, pp. 310–311.
66. John Paul II, *Gift and Mystery*, Random House, New York 1996, pp. 88–89.
67. Conchita Cabrera De Armida, *Sacerdoti di Cristo*, Città Nuova, Rome 2008, pp. 68–69.
68. Klaus Hemmerle, *Scelto per gli uomini*, Città Nuova, Rome 1995, p. 108.
69. Mahatma Gandhi, in René Voillaume, *Come loro*, Paoline, Rome 1963, p. 93.
70. Edith Stein, *La preghiera della Chiesa*, Brescia 1987, p. 23.
71. Gregory the Great, *Pastoral Rule*, I, 4.
72. John Henry Newman, *Parochial Sermons* IV, pp. 229–30.
73. Pope Benedict XVI, *The Angelus Message*, Castel Gandolfo 18 September 2005.
74. Mother Teresa of Calcutta, *For Love Alone: Reflections on Priestly Celibacy*, St. Pauls, Maynooth 1993, pp. 210–219, at pp. 213 and 217.
75. Cardinal Desmond Connell, *Christ Our Life*, Veritas, Dublin 1995, p. 136.
76. Card. Francis Xavier Van Thuan, *Testimony of Hope* (© Daughters of St. Paul. Used by permission of Pauline Books & Media, 50 St. Paul's Avenue, Boston, MA 02130. All rights reserved), p. 131.
77. Thomas McGovern, *Priestly Identity*, Four Courts Press, Dublin 2002, p. 20.
78. Card. Francis Xavier Van Thuan, *Testimony of Hope* (© Daughters of St. Paul. Used by permission of Pauline Books & Media, 50 St. Paul's Avenue, Boston, MA 02130. All rights reserved), p. 71.
79. Pope John Paul II, *Pastores Dabo Vobis*, n. 15.
80. Pope Benedict XVI, Chrism Mass, 9 April 2009.
81. Pope Benedict XVI, Chrism Mass, 9 April 2009.
82. Pope Paul VI, *Evangelii Nuntiandi*, 41.
83. Cardinal Carlo Maria Martini, *Lettera pastorale* 1999–2000, Milan 1999, pp. 12–13.
84. Pasquale Foresi, *Colloqui. Risposte sulla spiritualità dell'unità*, Città Nuova, Rome 2009, p. 73.
85. From *The Collected Works of Saint John of the Cross*, translated by Kieran Kavanaugh and Otilio Rodriguez. © 1964, 1979, 1991 by Washington Province of Discalced Carmelites, ICS Publications, 2131 Lincoln Rd., N.E., Washington, DC 20002-1199 U.S.A. www.icspublications.org.
86. 2008 Synod Message on the Word of God, n. 10, *Origins* 38 (2008), 341 349, at p. 346.
87. John Paul II, *Novo Millennio Ineunte*, 40.
88. Benedict XVI, To the Priests of the Diocese of Aosta (Italy), 25 July 2005.
89. Fulton Sheen, *The Priest Is Not His Own*, Ignatius Press, San Francisco 2004, p. 152.
90. Pope Benedict XVI, Answering a Question during His Flight to the United States 15 April 2008.
91. Card. Francis Xavier Van Thuan, *Testimony of Hope* (© Daughters of St. Paul. Used by permission of Pauline Books & Media, 50 St. Paul's Avenue, Boston, MA 02130. All rights reserved), pp. 78–79.
92. Chiara Lubich, "Il celibato sacerdotale," in *Città Nuova* 14 (1970/3) p. 9.
93. Cardinal Miloslav Vlk "The Spirituality of Diocesan Priests," in *Being One* (1996/5), pp. 61–72, at p. 66.
94. Benedict XVI, Homily at the Inaugural Mass of His Pontificate, 24 April 2005.

95. Hans Urs von Balthasar, *La realtà e la gloria*, Milan 1988, p. 54.
96. Saint Gregory the Great, "Homily II, Sunday after Easter," in *La teologia dei padri/4*, Città Nuova, Rome 1975, p. 128.
97. Giacomo Alberione, "Don Alberione ai sacerdoti," *Vita pastorale* (Supplement), dic. 1996, p. 101.
98. San Giovanni Maria Vianney, *Scritti scelti*, Città Nuova, Rome 1975, p. 94.
99. Silvano Cola, *Being One* 18 (2009/3), p. 40.
100. Card. Claudio Hummes, *Sempre discepoli di Cristo*, San Paolo, Milan 2002, p. 113.
101. Tom Lane, *Priesthood: Changeless & Changing*, Columba Press, Dublin 2005, p. 51.
102. Saint Josemaría Escrivá De Balaguer, *Christ Is Passing By*, Veritas, Dublin 1974, p. 117.
103. Stephen Rossetti, "Becoming Priests for the First Time," in *Origins*, 38 (2008), St. Luke Institute, Silver Spring, MD, 122–129, at p. 123.
104. Card. Francis Xavier Van Thuan, *Testimony of Hope* (© Daughters of St. Paul. Used by permission of Pauline Books & Media, 50 St. Paul's Avenue, Boston, MA 02130. All rights reserved), pp. 80–81.
105. G. K. Chesterton, *Orthodoxy*, The Bodley Head, London 1908, pp. 236–37.
106. Hubertus Blaumeiser, "Gesù abbandonato e la Chiesa", *Gen's* 36 (2006), p. 56
107. Quoted in *Finding Peace* © 2003 by Jean Vanier. Reprinted by permission of House of Anansi Press.
108. Klaus Hemmerle, "Decalogo del sacerdote," in *Gen's* 5 (1992), p. 182.
109. Pope Benedict XVI, Eucharistic Celebration with the New Cardinals, St. Peter's, Rome 25 March, 2006.
110. Chiara Lubich, "Priests for Today" in *Being One* 2 (1993) n. 2, pp. 2–12, at p. 11.
111. Bishop Klaus Hemmerle, *Scelto per gli uomini*, Città Nuova, Rome 1995, p. 43.
112. Silvano Cola, *Gen's*, 6 August 1971.
113. Hans Urs von Balthasar, *Elucidations*, Ignatius Press, San Francisco 1998, pp. 112–113.
114. Brendan Purcell, "*Fides et Ratio*: Charter for the Third Millennium," in James McEvoy (ed.), *The Challenge of Truth*, Veritas, Dublin 2002, pp. 240–253, at pp. 251–252.
115. Chiara Lubich, *Essential Writings*, New City Press, New York 2007, p. 140.
116. Enrico Pepe, *Martiri e santi*, Città Nuova, Rome 2006, pp. 472–473.
117. Don Tonino Bello, *Maria, donna dei nostri giorni*, San Paolo, Milan 1993, p. 96.
118. *Lumen Gentium*, 12.
119. Thomas O'Meara, *Theology of Ministry*, Paulist Press, New York 1999, p. 76.
120. Orthodox Patriarch Athenagoras, cited in Olivier Clément, *Dialogues avec le Patriarche Athénagoras*, Fayard, Paris 1969, p. 496.
121. Piero Coda, "Lo Spirito Santo crea la comunione," *Gen's* 21 (1991), pp. 193–194.
122. Hans Urs von Balthasar, *Prayer*, Ignatius Press, San Francisco 1986, 72–73, 79.
123. Copyright 2006, Benedictine Sisters, Mount St. Scholastica, Inc., Atchison, KS.

CPSIA information can be obtained at www.ICGtesting.com
Printed in the USA
BVOW070651240513

321534BV00001B/1/P